Stop All the Clocks, Cut Off the Telephone

Stop all the clocks, cut off the telephone,
Prevent the dog from barking with a juicy bone,
Silence the pianos and with muffled drum
Bring out the coffin, let the mourners come.

Let aeroplanes circle moaning overhead
Scribbling on the sky the message — He is Dead,
Put the crepe bows around the white necks of the public doves,
Let the traffic policemen wear black cotton gloves.

He was my North, my South, my East and West,
My working week and my Sunday rest,
My moon, my midnight, my talk, my song;
I thought that love would last forever: I was wrong.

The stars are not wanted now: put out every one;
Pack up the moon and dismantle the sun;
Pour away the ocean and sweep away the wood.
For nothing now can ever come to any good.

WH Auden

Saying Farewell to Those We Love

A Collection of Treasured Scripture, Poetry and Prose

JoJo
PUBLISHING

Barry H. Young

Sequel to The Funeral Celebrant's Handbook

Saying Farewell to Those We Love
Barry H. Young
Published by JoJo Publishing
First published 2011
'Yarra's Edge'
2203/80 Lorimer Street
Docklands VIC 3008
Australia
Email: jo-media@bigpond.net.au or visit www.jojopublishing.com

JoJo
PUBLISHING

JoJo Publishing
Designer / typesetter: Chameleon Print Design
Printed in China by Everbest Printing

National Library of Australia Cataloguing-in-Publication entry

Author:	Young, Barry H.
Title:	Saying farewell to those we love / Barry H. Young.
Edition:	1st ed.
ISBN:	9780987073488 (hbk.)
Series:	Young, Barry H., Funeral Celebrant's Handbook : no. 2
Subjects:	Funeral rites and ceremonies--Handbooks, manuals, etc.
Other Authors/	
Contributors:	Editor: Harris, Ormé.
Dewey Number:	393.9

Contents

Preface: The Aim of the Funeral Passages

The main purpose of this book is to provide practising and aspiring celebrants, a selection of poems, prose and phrases to assist with every manner of a loved one's passing. There are passages for the elderly, middle-aged, teenagers, babies, tragic occurrences, suicides and lonely; those who cut themselves off from society; those without family and those affected by illnesses and drugs. It provides tributes from husbands and wives, tributes from sons and daughters, grandchildren and those who served in the forces, together with religious readings and prayers.

It is not a working reference manual similar to the 'Funeral Celebrant's Handbook'; however, it complements it with a myriad of appropriate alternative passages that challenge funeral celebrants to be proactive in providing a choice of enhanced funeral rites. How often does a celebrant use the same tired dialogue avoiding words that might sound flowery or archaic, yet whose meaning, depth of understanding, empathy and beauty, bring solace, comfort and a sense of closure to the bereaved? No doubt when preparing and conducting a service we all have our own styles, creativity and sensitivity in the final presentation. This book of passages is not meant to change one's own unique technique, but to offer an abundance of alternative or inspirational choices.

Being mindful of order and clarity I have endeavoured to keep this large selection of poems, prose and readings uncluttered. Accordingly I have placed appropriate passages under specific headings. The headings are in similar order and sequence to 'The Funeral Celebrant's Handbook' commencing with the Introduction and culminating with the Committal and Benediction.

I hope this work will inspire and encourage my fellow celebrants to aspire to greater heights of excellence in offering a meaningful service to provide comfort, understanding and peace to the bereaved.

As the Master, Dally Messenger, said, 'The main challenge is the development of the culture by the best use of poetry, prose, music and symbols from all sources. Ultimately this must result in a much improved quality of marking and celebrating important occasions.'

This book is also targeted to assist any individuals wishing to participate in a funeral ceremony, so they too may appropriately select material for individual and specific circumstances. Poetry has historically expressed one's deepest feelings in the most moving and effective artistry; therefore let us have the courage to use such material to its ultimate advantage!

About the Author

Barry H Young OAM is a registered and experienced funeral celebrant. His book *The Funeral Celebrant's Handbook* has been widely acclaimed here in Australia, as well as internationally, as a valuable reference. It is an inspiring training manual and guide to those wishing to enter this significant and caring ministry.

Barry is an author of historical literature and is also Australia's most prominent author of Western Frontier novels, *River of Dreams, Reign of Terror, Shadows on the Lonesome Trail* and *The Undefeated* being some of his best-known works. His writings include award winning short stories — *Shadows of the Wolf, The Snake Trail* and *Red Wind* which have been described as 'pure poetry'.

Barry has been a member of the Australian Federation of Civil Celebrants since 1998. Being mindful of grief and the provision of comfort to young and old on his journey as a funeral celebrant, he has been compelled to share some of his experiences. His uniquely structured services impact on any assembly, as he views death as a transition from this world to the next, as an event to be celebrated in a dignified and proper manner. To hear him present a Farewell or Memorial Service is to be amongst the privileged.

Barry received the 'Order of Australia' award for recognition of meritorious service to the community supporting a range of youth services, aged care, disadvantaged and underprivileged people as well as grief counselling.

He lives with his wife Bev, and family, in the beautiful Thurgoona Valley in NSW.

Passage 1   A Heartfelt Opening

*D*eath arrives unannounced and is often a shock to those left behind. It is mysterious and bewildering to some. Death makes one ponder and reflect on all aspects of the individual's contribution to the world, and how best to say 'Farewell'. Some feel saddened or uncomfortable with its repercussions, some feel relief that the loved one is no longer in pain, whilst others are so stricken with grief or shock, they find immense difficulty in coping. It is therefore the caring funeral celebrant who can ease the pain, structure a fitting farewell, provide respectful support during this traumatic period and contribute by preparing the most fitting and appropriate ceremony. A celebration of the individual's life, whether momentous or trivial, brief or substantial, is of intrinsic importance and value to the family or loved ones. Advisedly, an opening verse to commence proceedings, and subtly establish a feeling of comfort, is essential to set the right tone for the service. I sincerely hope that in perusing the following pages, you may be inspired to ably cope with many different situations, and confidently present the most appropriate farewells.

Serenity Prayer

God, grant us the …
Serenity to accept things we cannot change,
Courage to change the things we can, and the
Wisdom to know the difference
Patience for the things that take time
Appreciation for all that we have, and
Tolerance for those with different struggles
Freedom to live beyond the limitations of our past ways, the
Ability to feel your love for us and our love for each other and the
Strength to get up and try again even when we feel it is hopeless.

Reinhold Niebuhr

Or

Love doesn't end with dying
Or leave in the last breath
For someone you've loved deeply
Love goes on forever.

Or

I ask not wealth
Nor length of days
Nor pride nor power
Nor worldly praise.
But just a little quiet place
Where a friend may come.
Laying their hand on the door.
As though it were home
For love doesn't end with dying.
Or leave in the last breath
For someone you've loved deeply
Love goes on forever.

Adaptation by Barry H Young

Passage 2   Always in Our Hearts

*S*ensitivity is important throughout a funeral ceremony. The atmosphere at a gathering may initially be paralysing to the bereaved. It may also be frightening or painful as full impact of purpose is felt. Commencing a ceremony with compassion and understanding is therefore vitally necessary. The following are thoughts on life and death which may softly minimise the feelings of bewilderment.

For an elderly lady

They say it's a beautiful journey
From the old World to the new
Some day we'll all take that journey
Up the stairway that leads to you.
And when we reach that garden of beautiful fragrant flowers.
Where all are filled with joy and peace and love
For God looked around his garden and found an empty space
He then looked down upon the earth
And found a lovely gracious lady
A golden heart had stopped beating
Two hands were laid to rest
He put his arms around you Joyce
And lifted you to rest.
Now that garden must be beautiful.
Because He only takes the best.

Author unknown

For an elderly gentleman

In a sea-blue harbour two ships sailed.
One setting off on a voyage.
The other coming home to port.
Every one cheered the ship going out
But the ship sailing in was hardly noticed.
To this the wise man replied
Do not rejoice over a ship setting out to sea
For you cannot know what terrible storm it may endure.
Rejoice over the ship that has safely reached its port
And brings its passengers home in peace.
And this is the way of the world.
When a child is born we all rejoice
When someone dies we all grieve.
But you and I, we should do the opposite for none of us can tell
What trials and tribulations await the newborn child.
For when a loved one dies in peace
We should rejoice for (Name) who has completed a long, meaningful
And worthwhile journey.

Author unknown

That Man Is a Success

That man is a success
Who has lived well
Laughed often and given much
Who gained the respect of others
And the love of children.
Who has filled his destiny and accomplished his tasks.
Who has left a treasure book of memories.
Who leaves this world a better place than he found it.
Who has never lacked appreciation in others or failed to express it.
Who looked for the best in others and gave the best that he had.

Adapted from Bessie A Stanley,
'What Constitutes Success'

The Hand of God

When we lose a loved one
Our world just falls apart.
We think that we can't carry on
With this broken heart.
Everything is different now
You're upset and you're annoyed.
Your world it seems is shattered
There's such an awful void.
There's got to be a reason
And we have to understand.

Author unknown

A reading for a death in tragic circumstances

Many services are imbued with extreme grief and sadness — the deaths of young people, tragic accidents, suicides, and so on. Sometimes the sadness felt may be quite intense. You may thus begin the service by asking everyone for courage and strength to bond together for the duration of the ceremony and beyond, to help one another through their pain.

You are Stronger than You Think

Within you is the strength to meet life's challenges
You are stronger than you think.
Remember to stand tall
Every challenge in your life helps you to grow
Every problem you encounter strengthens your mind and your soul
Every trouble you overcome increases your understanding of life
When all your troubles weigh heavily on your shoulders
Remember that beneath the burden you can stand tall
Because you are never given more than you can handle
And you — are stronger than you think.

> *Adapted from Lisa Wroble:*
> *Within You Is the Strength to Meet Life's Challenges*

Life is a Journey

For each of us here today, life is a journey.
It is a journey in time.
Our birth is the beginning of that journey
And it is important to believe that death is not the end but the destination.
For our life is a journey that takes us from youth to age
From innocence to awareness
From ignorance to knowledge
From foolishness to wisdom
From weakness to strength and often back again.
It takes us from offence to forgiveness
From loneliness to friendship
From pain to compassion
From fear to faith — from defeat to victory.
But it's not until we look backwards or look ahead
That we see that victory does not lie at some point along the way
But in having made the journey, step by step
Stage by stage
Has made that journey and made it well.

Author unknown

Remember Me

To the sorrowful, I will never return
To the angry, I was cheated
But to the happy, I am at peace
And to the faithful, I have never left
I cannot be seen, but I can be heard.
So as you stand upon a shore, gazing at a beautiful sea — remember me.
As you look in awe at a mighty forest and its grand majesty — remember me.
As you look upon a flower and admire its simplicity — remember me.
Remember me in your heart, your thoughts, and your memories of the times we loved,
the times we cried, the times we fought, the times we laughed
For if you always think of me, I will have never gone.

Author unknown

Life is but a Stopping Place

Life is but a stopping place
A pause in what's to be
A resting place along the road
to sweet eternity.
We all have different journeys
Different paths along the way
We all were meant to learn some things
But never meant to stay
Our destination is a place
Far greater than we know.
For some the journey's quicker
For some the journey's slow.
And when the journey finally ends
We'll claim a great reward
And find an everlasting peace
Together with the Lord.

Author unknown

There is No Death

There is a plan far greater than the plan you know.
There is a landscape broader than the one you see.
There is a haven where storm-tossed souls may go —
You call it death — we, immortality.
You call it death — this seeming endless sleep;
We call it birth — the soul at last set free.
'Tis hampered not by time or space — you weep.
Why weep at death? 'Tis immortality.
Farewell, dear voyager — 'twill not be long.
Your work is done — now may peace rest with thee.
Your kindly thoughts and deeds — they will live on.
This is not death — 'tis immortality.
Farewell, dear voyager — the river winds and turns;
The cadence of your song wafts near to me,
And now you know the thing that all men learn:
There is no death — there's immortality.

Author unknown

A Life Well Lived

A life well lived is a precious gift of hope, and strength and grace
From someone who has made our world a brighter, better place.
It's filled with moments sweet and happy with smiles and sad sometimes with tears.
Then there were friendships formed and good times shared and layered through the years.
A life well lived is a legacy of joy and pride and pleasure,
A loving lasting memory of grateful hearts and pleasure,
A Loving lasting memory our grateful hearts will treasure

Author unknown

Other

There are many suitable poems written by Helen Steiner Rice which can be used for an opening from the following books. *Just For You — Loving Thoughts — And the Greatest of These is Love — A Time to Love — Lovingly — Thankfully — Heart Gifts.*

Light-Hearted Verse

There is a short, wonderful, witty poem written by Joyce Grenfell: *If I Should Go Before the Rest of You*, which is ideal for reminding mourners of the deceased's love of life and fun under any circumstance. Copyright © Richard Scott Simon Pty Ltd.

Passage 3   Deeply Loved

There is no way to exist in this world, than to accept loss, for it is inevitable. Loss can be sudden, tragic, unwarranted, accidental, calculated or providential. Whatever the reason, the frame of mind of those closest to the individual can be fraught with disbelief or incredulity. Some may appear frozen and in need of assistance to discuss the death openly and frankly. It is the only way to assess what you, the instrument in that celebration can provide. Death brings a new perspective on life, and it is vital to sift what is worthy and what is worthless, the significant happenings in that life span and its comforting conclusion. The sense of peace and calmness provided during the celebration of that individual life sets the right tone. Following the Introduction another verse or reading is therefore recommended.

Grief

Grief is not a mountain to be climbed,
With the strong reaching the summit
Long before the weak.
Grief is not an athletic event,
With stop watches timing our progress.
Grief is a walk through loss and pain
With no competition and no time limits.

Do Not Grieve

When I am dead my dearest,
Sing no sad songs for me,
Plant thou no roses at my head,
Nor shady cypress tree.
Be the green grass above me
With showers and dewdrops wet,
And if thou wilt, remember,
And if thou wilt, forget.
I shall not see the shadows,
I shall not feel the rain,
I shall not hear the nightingale
Sing on, as if in pain.
And dreaming through the twilight
That doth not rise nor set.
Haply I may remember
And haply not forget.

Christina Rossetti

A Place in Heaven

There is a place in Heaven for everyone to go,
God also has a garden where the very best blooms grow.
He looked around the garden and saw an empty space.
So he gently took our mother's hand and said, 'This is your place.'
So keep it in your heart,
That even though she's gone,
She's in that special garden,
Where God's best blooms belong
For he only takes the best.
Remember all the good times.
Be happy for her 'Smile'.

Author unknown

Untitled

Hold on to what is good
Even if it is
A handful of earth
Hold on to what you believe
Even if it is
A tree which stands by itself
Hold on to what you must do
Even if it is
A long way from here
Hold on to life even when
It is easier letting go
Hold on to my hand even when
I have gone from you

Copyright © Nancy Wood

Untitled

Let me die working
Still tackling plans unfinished, tasks undone!
Clean to its end, swift may my race be run.
No lagged steps, no faltering, no shirking;
Let me die working!
Let me die thinking.
Let me fare forth still with an open mind.
Fresh secrets to unfold, new truths to find,
My soul undimmed, alert, no questions blinking;
Let me die thinking! Let me die, giving!
The substance of life for life's enriching;
Time, things, and self on heaven converging,
No selfish thought, loving, redeeming. Living;
Let me die giving.

S Hall Young

When I Am Gone

When I am gone, if I shall go before you
Think of me not as a disconsolate lover.
Think of the joy it gave me to adore you.
Of sun, and the stars you helped me to discover.
And this still living part of me
Will come to sit beside you in the empty room.
Then all on earth that death has left behind
Will be merry part of me within your mind.

Author unknown

I'm Still Here

Friend, please don't mourn for me
I'm still here, though you don't see.
I'm right by your side each night and day
And within your heart I long to stay.
My body is gone but I'm always near.
I'm everything you feel, see or hear.
My spirit is free, but I'll never depart
As long as you keep me alive in your heart.
I'll never wander out of your sight —
I'm the brightest star on a summer night.
I'll never be beyond your reach —
I'm the warm moist sand when you're at the beach.
I'm the colourful leaves when Autumn's around
And the pure white snow that blankets the ground.
I'm the beautiful flowers of which you're so fond,
The clear cool water in a quiet pond.
I'm the first bright blossom you'll see in the spring,
The first warm raindrop that April will bring.
I'm the first ray of light when the sun starts to shine,
And you'll see that the face in the moon is mine.
When you start thinking there's no one to love you,
You can talk to me through the Lord above you.
I'll whisper my answer through the leaves on the trees,
And you'll feel my presence in the soft summer breeze.
I'm the hot salty tears that flow when you weep
And the beautiful dreams that come while you sleep.
I'm the smile you see on a baby's face.
Just look for me, friend, I'm every place!

Author unknown

When We Lose Someone

When we lose someone dear to us the hurt can be almost unbearable —
Yet I know somehow we will get through it.
I believe that it is because we feel such pain —
Because the inner ache is so great, that we realise how much we loved Ken.
Yet the hurt inside gives us a strange comfort.
It is telling us just how much we loved him.
Because the grief and heartache we feel bears witness to the depths of our love.
You see grief is a great indicator and measure of love.
It simple cannot and does not exist except where there has been love.
So it is in thinking of Ken today and saying goodbye for the time being
That we can say thank you to Ken and celebrate a life well lived.

Barry H Young

Some words of comfort

Beyond the beautiful sunset,
Free from all sorrow and pain
Our lives will be lonely without you
In our hearts you will always remain.
There is sunshine for each sunset
And for each night of sorrow.
There is an ending as the new day dawns
On the horizon called tomorrow.
Don't cry because Helen has gone away
But smile because Helen was here.

Author unknown

I look around today and unlike most funerals services that I conduct there are more young people than we oldies so may I just share with you a word on grief.

Many people that I talk to believe that being strong and brave about a lost loved one means trying to think and talk about something else. But we know that being strong and brave means thinking and talking about our lost one.

Be Strong and Brave

The name of your lost one is a magic word.
Did you know?
Wherever you are, whether busy or relaxing
Think, talk, speak the name — Shayne.
Then whatever happens
Let it happen,
Even if it be tears.
You see it's okay to cry as it is to laugh.
The name of your loved one or friend is a magic word … Shayne.
Speak it — think it.
This, until your grief begins to be bearable and heal.
Now that is strength.
That is courage and only thus can 'Being Strong and Brave' help you to heal.

Author unknown

Remember Me in Your Hearts

Remember the music, the songs played sometimes,
Play them again — let them resonate in your minds.
Remember picnics, BBQs, and long summer days
Roll out the mem'ries —
Remember growing years, the passion and laughter —
They will remain — my own 'ever after.'
I encountered a cross-road — the purpose seemed blurred
A darkened roller-coaster — I climbed aboard
It just happened — I'm sorry … now that door is closed.

If you pause for a while and quietly reminisce
The many frustrations — that made you all hiss!
They were part of my growth, my foibles and frailties
They were part of my makeup, my disabilities
I did not mean to make you mad —
I did not mean to make you sad —
Accept my humble apologies!
I was present here — for just a space in time.
My farewell call came early — sadly marked as 'mine'

I love you all dearly — please do rest assured
I could not express it — my words they went unheard …
We'll meet again somewhere — beyond that far rise …
I'm flying — I'm at peace — I'm in my own paradise!

When a Good Person Dies

Night is coming on.
The last birds fly hurriedly to their nests.
Slowly but surely darkness takes possession of the world.
However, no sooner has darkness fallen,
than the lights begin to come on —
below us, around us, above us,
near us and far away from us —
a candle in a window, a lamp in a cellar,
a beacon in a lighthouse, a star in the sky.
And so we take heart and find our way again.
When a good person dies, darkness descends on us.
We feel lost, bereft, forlorn.
But gradually the lights begin to come on
as we recall the good deeds done by the deceased.
They spring up all over the place.
We are amazed at how much light is generated.
In this strange and beautiful light
we not only find our way,
but find the meaning of life itself.

Author unknown

I Am Free

Don't grieve for me, for now I'm free,
I'm following paths God made for me
I took his hand, I heard him call
Then turned, and bid farewell to all.
I could not stay another day
To laugh, to love, to sing, to play
Tasks left undone must stay that way
I found my peace … at close of play.

And if my parting left a void
Then fill it with remembered joy
A friendship shared, a laugh, a kiss
Ah yes, these things I too will miss.
Be not burdened … deep with sorrow
I wish you sunshine of tomorrow
My life's been full; I've savoured much
Good friends, good times
A loved one's touch.

Perhaps my time seemed all too brief
Don't lengthen it now with grief
Lift up your heart and share with me
God wants me now … He set me free.
(or alternative last line: The joy of love and life — for now I'm free.)

Author unknown

To Those I Love

If I should ever leave you whom I love
To go along the silent Way, grieve not,
Nor speak of me with tears, but laugh and talk
Of me as if I were beside you there,
(I'd come... I'd come, could I but find a way!
But would not tears and grief be barriers?)
And when you hear a song, or see a bird I loved,
Please do not let the thought of me be sad ...
For I am loving you just as I always have ...
You were so good to me!
There are so many things I wanted still to do ...
So many things to say to you ...
Remember that I did not fear ...
It was just leaving you that was so hard to face ...
We cannot see Beyond ... But this I know:
I loved you so ...
'Twas heaven here with you!

Isla Paschal Richardson
Read by Gregory Peck at Frank Sinatra's funeral.

Turn Again to Life

If I should die and leave you here a while,
Be not like others, sore undone, who keep
Long vigils by the silent dust, and weep.
For my sake — turn again to life and smile,
Nerving thy heart and trembling hand to do
Something to comfort other hearts than thine.
Complete those unfinished tasks of mine,
And I, perchance, may therein comfort you.

Mary Lee Hall
Read by Lady Sarah McCorquodale, eldest sister of Princess Diana, at Princess Diana's funeral.

God Saw You Getting Tired

God saw you getting tired,
When a cure was not to be.
So He wrapped his arms around you,
And whispered, 'Come to me.'
You didn't deserve what you went through,
So He gave you rest.
God's garden must be beautiful,
He only takes the best
And when I saw you sleeping,
So peaceful and free from pain
I could not wish you back
To suffer that again —

Author unknown

Passage 4   So Dearly Loved, So Sadly Missed

Partners, particularly those who have travelled together for many years, shared the burdens of family life, endured the unimaginable and bonded inseparably, would find it hard to bear the loss of their partner. Providing the most appropriate wording to elucidate that bond is therefore important. Words can paint the picture and portray the life shared so intimately. All the substantial things that are meaningful in life, such as music, conversation, eating, dancing, playing with children, walking, etc., can thus be spoken of and shared with the gathering, emphasising the individual's contribution to all manner of things. The following passages are special and enlighten the gathering as to the immensity of that love and the loss in its immediacy.

A reading from a wife
who dearly loved her husband

Memories

When I have slipped into the past, I'd like you to recall
Not the deeds I won or lost, not that way at all
I'd like you to remember, all the love I shared with you
A love that started tender, a love so young and true
You found me. I was just a child, emerging into woman
You taught me love, strange and strong, surely made in heaven
You guided and encouraged me; you showed me what was best
And I in turn, gave you my dreams — from my treasure chest
A mother, wife, a lover true, you wanted all of me
Each passing year I focused on — who I should really be
Our life, our home, our children, they filled my every scheme
And you were there — my cornerstone, in every plan and scene
Photographs that we compiled — there's stories on every page
Our life thus captured lovingly, if memories ever fade
For those we love can never be — more than a thought apart
And we belong, you and me — so keep me close forever in your heart

Copyright © Ruth Van Gramberg

Should You Go First

Should you go first and I remain
To walk the road alone,
I'll live in memory's garden, dear,
With happy days we've known.
In spring I'll wait for roses red,
When fades the lilac blue,
In early fall, when brown leaves call
I'll catch a glimpse of you.
Should you go first and I remain
For battles to be fought,
Each thing you've touched along the way
Will be a hallowed spot.
I'll hear your voice, I'll see you smile,
Though blindly I may grope,
The memory of your helping hand
Will buoy me on with hope.

Should you go first and I remain
To finish with the scroll,
No length'ning shadows shall creep in
To make this life seem droll.
We've known so much of happiness,
We've had our cup of joy,
And memory is one gift of God
That death cannot destroy.

Should you go first and I remain,
One thing I'd have you do:
Walk slowly down that long, lone path,
For soon I'll follow you.
I'll want to know each step you take,
That I may walk the same,
For someday down that lonely road
You'll hear me call your name.

AK Rowswell

Forever in My Heart

The man/woman I love is missing,
A voice I love is still.
A place is vacant in my heart
That no one else can fill.

No matter how my life may change
Or whatever I may do,
I will always cherish the memories,
Of the years I spent with you,
Forever in my heart.

Author unknown

You Never Said Goodbye

You never said I'm leaving
You never said goodbye.
You were gone before I knew it,
And only God knew why.
A million times I needed you,
A million times I cried.
If love alone could have saved you,
You never would have died.
In life I loved you dearly,
In death I love you still.
In my heart you hold a place,
That no one could ever fill.
It broke my heart to lose you,
But you didn't go alone
For part of me went with you,
The day God took you home.

Author unknown

Helen had a deep love for her family and countless friends and the following words are a tribute to that enduring unconditional love

To be loved truly by someone is a rare thing.
A Wife's love, A Husband's love, a Mother and Father's love, a Grandparent's love
And a friend's love is something that is never lost.
It is a love that can't be described.
If love is one thing that can be passed down from generation to generation
Then Helen you have done your job
For the love that was in your heart is now in ours and we can never forget you.
Your love surrounds us every day.
You are part of us forever.
We love you Helen
Rest in Peace.

Author unknown

Joan and Norman shared a wonderful togetherness; they were soul-mates and the following is a tribute to that togetherness

One day my darling I will join you.
When my life on earth is through.
Until that day my darling
I will go on loving you.
When I think about the happiness.
That you and I shared.
And all the things you've said and done.
To show how much you cared.
Although we seldom mentioned it.
We both knew it was true.
We had the kind of happiness.
Life gives to very few.
A togetherness and home that we both cherished.
Children, family and friends we held dear.
And love for one another.
That grew deeper every year.

Author unknown

Don loved his garden and these are some beautiful words that I say to Don from Dorothy

Finding You in Beauty

The rays of light filtered through
The sentinels of trees this morning.
I sat in the garden and contemplated.
The serenity and beauty
Of my feelings and surroundings
Completely captivated me.
I thought of you.
I discovered you tucked away
In the shadows of the trees.
Then, rediscovered you
In the smiles of the flowers
As the sun penetrated their petals
In the rhythm of the leaves
Falling in the garden
In the freedom of the birds
As they fly searching as you do.
I'm very happy to have found you,
Now you will never leave me
For I will always find you in the beauty of life.

Walter Rinder

A beautiful reading that depicts one's love for another

Untimely Loss

For all the years we had you to ourselves
Now they seem — far too short awhile
As joyously we came to really love you
Your special hugs, often brought a smile
Your helpful ways — they touched us all so deeply
Your daily actions proudly held intent
Ambitions, goals — that you would one day savour
Those dreams alas, were for a short time lent
Plans designed — they suddenly all perished
Leaving souvenirs — drenched with many a tear
Saddened hearts — each tender moment cherished
Concealed emptiness — a burden hard to bear.
We did but glimpse, a fleeting touch of heaven
The privilege of having known you now sustains
Your gentle spirit touched so many loved ones
Images, smiles and melodies swamp unlimited
Like fragrant leaves and petals — they remind
Your face and smile — all lovingly remembered
In each and every heart you left behind
We thank you for having spent some time with us.
Goodbye (Name) our loved one, for now it's time to say farewell.
The echo of your footsteps now remains
But now it's time to gently — softly — close the door.

Tomorrows

After this day has darkened and gone
And I wake to the rest of my life
I shall think of the times and the places we saw
When we were husband and wife.
And I know I shall visit those places we loved
And walk by the fields and the sea
Where you and I spent our happiest hours
And somehow you'll be there with me.

If I go through the woods to the top of the hill
Or run barefoot over the sand
I shall hear your voice in the wind, my love,
And feel the touch of your hand.
And people who see me on my own
As they pass me on the track
Might wonder why, if I'm really alone,
As I pause sometimes and look back.

To where the roadside trees are blurred
By the early evening mist
I'll be waiting for you to catch up, my love,
From where you've stopped to rest.
And though people will find many ways to be kind
They will never quite understand
How I hear your voice in the sigh of the wind
And feel the touch of your hand.

Simon Bridges

Five Candles for (Name)

The first candle represents joy
The pain of losing you is with us now
However we are reminded of the joyous times
Spent with you — the happiest moments in our lives
And all you meant to our family.
We will always miss you.
(Name) — will light the first candle.

The second candle represents courage
To confront our sorrow
To comfort each other and to remind us
That you faced many hardships and battles
And yet had a smile for all your loved ones.
(Name) — will light the second candle.

The third candle we light in your memory
For the times we laughed, the times we cried
The times we were angry at the silly things you did
How we learned to love your laughter and silly jokes
Most of all — your loving hugs at all times
(Name) — will light the third candle.

The fourth candle we light for all the love we received
For the beautiful memories we have of you
For your warm presence — the special meals you cooked
The yummy cakes and the love extended
At family gatherings.
(Name)— will light the fourth candle.

The fifth candle is to thank you for the gift of life
You brought us into this world — and we are grateful.
Whenever we look at each other or our loved ones
We will see a part of you in them — a living legacy of your touch.
We will remember the good times and the not so good times
And all the special moments shared with you.
We will love you forever!!
(Name) — will light the fifth candle.

Copyright © Ruth Van Gramberg

Ken and Mary shared a wonderful marriage and togetherness and these few words are a tribute to that wonderful happening

If Two Are Caring (or Marriage is Love)

If two are caring, as they're sharing life's hopes and fears
If the music of laughter outweighs sadness of tears
Then marriage is togetherness.
If both derive pleasure from mere presence of each other
Yet when parted no jealousies restrict, worry or smother
Then marriage is freedom.
If achievements mean more when they benefit two
And consideration is shown with each point of view
Then marriage is respect.
And if togetherness, freedom and respect are combined
With a joy that words can never fully define
Then marriage is love.

Author unknown

I Miss You

When I think of you, I remember so many things
A rain-washed street, a book, a fireplace
A comfy chair to rest
Photos abound of green hills and vales
Planned holidays or trips
A welcome at the station
Those journeys home — the best
I see a simple table laid, with candles lit for two
Food and wine — fit for the gods
It seemed so right with you
As summer fades, and winter calls
Winds roar through the night
Your armchair is still my 'welcome home'
Your slippers red and bright
When evening falls, and night descends
Darkness then curtains my nest
I close my eyes on pillow warm
A place my head to rest
But you invade my every dream
And softly sing 'our song'
Oh, how I miss you!!

Some beautiful thoughts that make death
a little easier to understand

You Tried So Hard

You tried so hard, you told so few,
With tears we saw you suffer,
We watched you fade away,
Our hearts were slowly breaking,
As you fought so hard to stay,
You did not want to leave us,
But you did not go alone,
For part of us went with you,
The day God called you home.

Author unknown

My Heart Aches with Sadness

My heart aches with sadness,
My secret tears flow,
For what it means to lose you,
No one will ever know.
Our thoughts are always with you,
Your place no one will fill,
In life we loved you dearly,
In death we love you still.
The things we feel so deeply,
Are the hardest things to say,
But you will always be remembered,
In a very special way.

Author unknown

Reading from a Bereaved Wife

To hear your voice, to see your smile,
To sit and talk with you a while,
To be together in the same old way,
Would be my only wish today,
We laugh, we cry, we play our part
But behind it all lies a broken heart,
We hide our tears when we speak your name,
Without you … life's not the same.

Author unknown

Passage 5   Our Everlasting
Cherished Memories

*T*he loss of a beloved family member is traumatic whatever the circumstances. No one can assuage the loss, or experience the heartbreaking distress felt by the bereaved family. That book of life requires its chapters revisited, brought into the sunshine and evaluated in all its joys or frailties. This passage is therefore dedicated to bidding farewell to sons, daughters, mothers, fathers, grandparents, or grandchildren. The readings provided here may assist the celebrant in selecting words to aptly suit the particular individual.

Coping with the loss of a child, son or daughter is horrific. The smiles, the laughter, the pain, the insecurities of the individual vibrate in a deafening manner. Finding the right words is often difficult.

When you feel Lonely

When a person you love passes away
Look to the night sky on a clear day.
The star that to you, appears to be bright,
Will be your loved one,
Looking upon you during the night.
The lights of heaven are what shows through
As your loved one watches all that you do.
When you feel lonely for the one that you love,
Look to the Heavens in the night sky above.

Author unknown

Are You There?

Misty breeze wraps about my shoulders, thinly clad.
I shiver not, despite the coolness of my skin.
Comfort, I now feel.
Is it you my precious Angel?
Are you there? I cannot hear your quiet voice,
But bird song fills the air
From high treetops to grassy marsh.
I wonder — is it you, dear? Are you there?
The roses in your garden bloom large,
And varied in hue from crimson deep, to barely pink.
I cup the velvet bud; its fragrance soothes a troubled mind.
This must be you, my little girl. Are you there?
Are you the fiery autumn maples,
Or the star-like flakes of snow?
Are you the sparkle in the water of the lake that we both loved,
Or, perhaps, the warmth I feel in the sand beneath my toes?
Though your quiet voice I cannot hear,
Nor can I see again your sparkling eyes,
Or feel your dainty hand laid gently on my own,
You are here.
For memory's book will never close —
Each lovely sound, or sight, or scent,
another page from special times that we have shared.
Oh, yes! You are here child — everywhere!

Diane Robertson

My Beloved Katie

Each day I wake up from a terrible dream
Only to find the world has changed.
I go to your room; your things are still there
Your dolls, your medals and your favourite bear.
The scent of you lingers, the smell of your hair
Memories of you, I find, are everywhere.
Your precious books are stacked by the bed
And tissues that captured your tears as you read.
Your paintings and drawings still hang on the wall
Collections of seashells and rocks from the beach
Bring back the memories of the times well spent.
How do I go on without you by my side,
To love you to hold you, with smiles and pride?
My heart, it is broken, my dear beloved child.
I miss your laughter, your music and your smiles,
All of our dreams of the future will never come true
The 'whys' and 'if onlys' endlessly swirl in my head
Please tell me, oh God, I wish I were dead.
I want to be with you every second of the day
But Dad and your sister, they need me to stay
Your friends and your family will never forget,
Your friendship, your love and your gentle kindness.
You will live on forever in their hearts and their mind
I will love you forever my darling, my child.

Jason's Gift

When you left
You took the cool breeze of summer with you.
Rainbows paled
Smiles became grimaces
And the air I sucked into my aching soul was fetid and thick.
Prayers became jokes
Faith turned to doubt
And hope lay buried under a rock.
Sunsets came in browns and greys, muted by the dullness in my soul.
Then you returned …
Swooping into my heart, transforming my reality
And bringing me truth —
A gift throbbing with the intensity of spirit.
Now rainbows pulse with brilliance,
Breezes rustle emerald leaves,
And the air I breathe gently cools my burning soul.
I understand that to know turquoise, I must first know grey.
And to know pink, I must understand brown.
I had to huddle in the black of an endless night
before I could grasp the radiance of a purple dawn.
Without sleep, there is no awakening.
Without darkness, no light.
And without knowing the desperate,
screaming agony of your death,
I did not know life.

> © *Sandy Goodman*
> Author of *Love Never Dies: A Mother's Journey from Loss to Love*
> (Jodere 2002)

Tragic loss in car accident

If I Knew

If I knew it would be the last time that I'd see you fall asleep
I would tuck you in more tightly and pray the Lord, your soul to keep.
If I knew it would be the last time that I see you walk out the door,
I would give you a hug and kiss and call you back for one more.
If I knew it would be the last time I'd hear your voice lifted up in praise,
I would video tape each action so I could play them back day after day.
If I knew it would be the last time I could spare an extra minute,
To stop and say 'I LOVE YOU' instead of assuming you would know it.

Maybe there will always be — another day to say 'I love you',
And certainly another chance to say — 'Anything I can do?'
But just in case I might be wrong and today is all I get,
I'd like to say how much I love you and hope we never forget.
Tomorrow is not promised to anyone, young or old alike,
And today may be the last chance to hold your loved ones tight.
So if you're waiting for tomorrow, why not do it today?
For if tomorrow never comes, you'll surely regret this day.

That you didn't take extra time for a smile, a hug, or a kiss
And too busy to grant someone their one and only wish.
So hold your loved ones close today and whisper in their ear,
Tell them how much you love them and that you'll always hold them dear.
Often say: 'I'm sorry,' 'Please forgive me,' 'Thank You,' or 'It's OK.'
And if tomorrow never comes, you'll have no regrets about today.

Author unknown

Kerryn was a special Mum to Megan, Craig and Luke and the following words are a tribute to Kerryn

A mother is a wonderful creature constructed almost entirely of love.
And this she can express in a million ways.
From hugs and kisses and good cooking, and patient listening, to stern lectures,
Strict rules, and repeated uses of the word 'No'.
Like snowflakes, no two mothers are alike, but they have a number of things in common.
Name anything ... a mother can be found washing it, polishing it, getting rid of it, repairing it,
Spanking it, packing it, teaching it, redecorating it, loving it, or talking it over.
A mother cares about and for almost anything.
Gardens, pets, the state of the nation, the worn spot on the rug, hungry people,
And most of all her children.

Author unknown

Mothers Always Do

For those she loves she can do anything and fight for anything necessary to their happiness.
A mother is not always an angel.
She will often disagree with you ... expect too much of you ... question your choice of friends ...
And bring up the subject of work when you feel the least energetic.
But she's always ready to help when you need her.
You don't always tell a mother how much you love her, or how much you hope the most wonderful things in the world will come to her, because there are no words that express feelings so deep and sincere.
Somehow, though, you feel she understands what's in your heart.
Mother's always do!

Author unknown

My Mother

Mum, you were a shining example of love and all it encompassed. A beautiful human being — who touched the hearts of many, many people. This service here today is to honour and recognise the way in which you constantly enfolded individuals with your gentle warmth, friendship, love and generosity. You were also an immensely spiritual person, who believed in God and nurtured your family to love God and the miracle of life.

Mum, you were an outstanding lady. Quiet, in a shy sort of way, but with a character that remained strong, steadfast and honest. You were a very special lady that we feel has no equal. You were creative, gifted and artistic. Through the years, apart from being a mother to everyone, you patiently and painstakingly created gifts of love. There were delicate boxes adorned with beautiful shells, paintings with flowers, exquisite etchings which were then — with love and a kiss — gifted to so many people who touched your life. You had a heart that was overflowing with love. Mother and matriarch, of our family.

Mum, you are no longer in pain; you are now with the angels and our dad. We can remember all the golden moments we have had with you and take comfort in the knowledge that your spirit can soar in the wind, dance amongst flowers, climb to the top of the mountains and whisper in the waves. Mum, you will always remain a part of us all. Every time we each look at our children, grandchildren, or great grandchildren, part of you is within us all. That is the continuity of life and you gave us life. We are grateful to God for having given you to us and decorated our lives with your goodness.

You were a queen amongst mothers and we will always love you and wish you farewell Mummy — rest in peace.

Copyright © Ruth Van Gramberg

My Children

My children, did I ever stop and tell you
How much I love you?
Each time I yelled
'Wipe your shoes before you come in the door;
Did you finish your homework?
Have you tidied your room?'
Those were but plaintive notes,
Ineptly saying — I truly care!
When I yelled —
'Turn that music down;
Wash up those dirty dishes;
Pick up those scattered books;
Don't forget your wallet!'
I was screaming I truly care!

Trying to convey my message
Within those boundaries of discipline —
Amidst the noise of your laughter and games
My heart was truly ablaze.
Perhaps as you grow older
And these aged phrases
Are repeated down the years
Your eyes may glisten with tears
As you hear —
The silent echo of my fears ...
'I love you' —
I'm still yelling — I truly care!

Copyright © Ruth Van Gramberg

For a beloved husband who shared in every little way

Canvas of My Love

I have often sat in pensive mood
And drawn a picture of you!
One who cared and loved and understood
Little complicated me.
You would listen with your heart
And feel my passion
Unspoken words — a chasm
Laid softly aside
Your dear face and hands
Indelibly etched inside.
The force that governed my life
And guided me to safety shores …
They still enfold!
You are not with me now
And yet … you are!
Shadows and dreams my cushions
Caressed by darkness
Loneliness and longings I cannot hide
This painting is you, my Love
I hang it gently in my heart
With pride!

Jim loved his family and the following reading describes his love of them

Being Part of a Family

Being part of a family is to acknowledge its roots
and all its extensions
To nurture an awareness of belonging, till the final
reluctant farewell
To ascertain the rhythms and heartbeats of life
as an unfolding constant
To acquire strong, steadfast values, virtues
and obligations
To have total confidence and trust
within stable and structured boundaries
To confront forgiveness, reconciliation, freshness
and love in abundance
To be a contributing equation manifesting
a cohesive foundation
To experience established familiar patterns
that resonate strength
To accept that sound relationships may sometimes
collapse and concede reform
To admit a child emerged from those special years
in worthy transformation
To sanction the essence of proud beliefs and tradition
bravely passed on
To joyously remember a multitude of endeavours
in the small corner of the world that will always be 'Home'!

Alf was much loved by his grandchildren and he adored them — the following words illustrate that love

Granddad, we want you to know that we loved you.
You were a very important part of our lives.
Our relationship, our memories and moments shared
And the love you've given us
Are all so very precious to us.
We count our blessings.
To have had a Granddad.
And we hope you realised that you have always been our inspiration.
You have guided us in each decision
And encouraged us to reach for every dream.
You have helped us through your guidance, wisdom and strength of your love
To become the persons you wanted us to be.
We want you to know that though we may not have told often enough
You mean so much more to us than words can say.
We thank you and we love you with all our hearts.
You were the greatest Granddad of all.

Author unknown

Arthur loved his grandchildren and they him and the following reading is from them

A wonderful Grandfather so loving and kind.
What beautiful memories you leave behind.
Sharing and caring and always content.
Loved and respected wherever you went.
A happy smile, a heart of gold.
You were the best this world could hold.
A special Grandfather so kind and true.
What beautiful memories we all have of you.

Author unknown

Our Poppy

We had a wonderful Poppy
One who never really grew old.
His smile was made of sunshine
And his heart was solid gold.
His eyes were bright as shining stars,
His cheeks touched by the sun
We had a wonderful Poppy,
And that's the way it will always be.
Then God looked around His garden
And saw an empty space.
He then looked down upon this earth
And saw Pop's smiling face.
God's garden must be beautiful
He always takes the best
And He chose our Pop to go there for a rest.
It broke our hearts to see him go
But he didn't go alone,
For part of us went with Pop
The day God called him home.
Each night we shed a silent tear,
As we speak to him in prayer
To let him know we love him
And just how much we cared.
Take our million teardrops
Wrap them up in love,
Then we ask the wind to carry them
To our Pop in heaven above.

Author unknown

*Barbara loved her grandchildren as they loved her —
and the following reading is from them*

*A wonderful grandmother so loving and kind.
What beautiful memories you leave behind.
Sharing and caring and always content.
Loved and respected wherever you went.
A happy smile; a heart of gold.
You were the best this world could hold.
A special grandmother so kind and true.
What beautiful memories we all have of you*

Author unknown

To a Nana

*A wife, a mother, a nana too
This legacy we have from you
You taught us love and how to fight
You gave us strength, you gave us might
A stronger person would be hard to find
And in your heart you were always kind
Not just a wife not just a mother, for all of us you gave your best
Now the time has come for you to rest
So go in peace, you've earned your sleep
Your love in our hearts, we'll eternally keep
We'll miss your smile; we'll miss your chats
Your smile, your chats we will never forget
We will hold them close to our hearts' content
You fought so hard to stay with us
However it was all too much
May your memories and stories keep going afar
Until we meet again
Love you always Nana.*

Author unknown

Our Nan

We had a wonderful Nan
One who never really grew old.
Her smile was made of sunshine
And her heart was solid gold.
Her eyes were bright as shining stars,
And in her cheeks fair roses you would see.
We had a wonderful Nan,
And that's the way it will always be.
Then God looked around His garden
And saw an empty space.
He then looked down upon this earth
And saw Nan's smiling face.
God's garden must be beautiful
He always takes the best
And He chose our Nan to go there for a rest.
It broke our hearts to see her go
But she didn't go alone,
For part of us went with Nan
The day God called her home.
Each night we shed a silent tear,
As we speak to her in prayer
To let her know we love her
And just how much we cared.
Take our million teardrops
Wrap them up in love,
Then we ask the wind to carry them
To our Nan in heaven above.

Author unknown

Passage 6   Loved Ones Re-united

There are some things in life we either do not comprehend, or wish for, yet receive ... sorrow in abundance! Accepting its force is often difficult and coming to terms with the torrent of remorse, bewilderment, pain and emptiness is often hard to attain. Finding the right words to portray this plethora of diverse emotions is often challenging, yet with patience and tenacity, this is achievable. Following are some beautiful thoughts that make death a little easier to understand and accept.

Don and Bobbie shared a wonderful marriage and togetherness and these few words are a tribute to that wonderful happening

Give the Love in Me Away

I want to leave you something
Far better than words can say
So look for me in the people I've known
Or helped in some special way
When the light of day in darkness is bound
Just think of the times we shared
And when you rise to a brand new day
With songs and music surround
There's many of you — I've talked to and loved
And held you with smiles and with praise
For love does not die — it lingers on
It's there in each sweet embrace
So when all that is left of me is love
Give love with a smile on your face
There's more of me to live on ... and on
In giving the love I gave to you.

When Life Comes to an End

When Life comes to an end, when all seasons are spent …
When death comes and claims its right, to say to me 'This is the End!'
I want to step through that door, full of curiosity, wondering
What is it going to be like … that unknown realm of obscurity?
I will then look upon the past, as no more than an idea — a fleeting span,
That started some yesterday and raced through years concealed.
When it's over, I want to say — Yes! Yes! That was me!!
I had gazed around with 'amazement', searching for answers
I lived, I breathed, I felt and touched. I followed many a dream!
And, when it's over, I don't want to wonder if I made my existence
Something particular, something unreal or something notable …
I don't want to leave ashamed or frightened, imploring 'one more day'!
To rectify some worthless deed …
I don't want to end up simply having visited this terrain and failed.
I want to leave — having stained it with my struggles, a palette of varied hues,
I shared, simply or expansively, wildly or silently, with payments and dues,
Life's complexities and triumphs hand in hand
As I did exist — from birth till now! And, it was 'Grand'!!
Pages brushed elusively with music, tears and mirth
I hungered for the unknown, and sought what touched my soul.
And proudly leave it 'Spectacular', for having lived and loved upon this earth!

Just a Number

We are just a number in life's big record book,
So there is no point in being scared
When it's our turn to look inside the gates of heaven
To see the great unknown
And meet with all our loved ones,
And never be alone.

Believing in the after-life
Will help you through the day,
For one thing's very certain:
Death will not go away.
But know that Heaven's waiting,
Your reward for work well done.
Look forward to the other side
Your new life's just begun.

Author unknown

A Universal Tribute

Though I depart this way,
A life unable to complete,
Your everlasting love will share,
Every moment in every day
Thoughts and memories, so few in time,
Yet special in every way
Will always travel in my mind,
Of a very special day
My love will always be with you,
As yours remains with me.
For this alone will see me through,
Until we meet another day.

Author unknown

God Sends His love

That day I had to leave you, when my life on earth was through,
God picked me up, hugged me and said
'I have big plans for you. I need you here so badly, as part of my big plan,
There's so much that we have to do to help our mortal man.'
Then God gave me a list of things, he wished me to do,
And foremost on that list of mine, is to watch and care for you.
To you, my dearest family, some things I'd like to say,
But first of all to let you know that I arrived OK
I'm writing this from heaven, where I dwell with God above
Where there're no more tears or sadness, there is just eternal love.
Please do not be unhappy, just because I'm out of sight,
Remember that I'm with you every morning, noon and night.
When you think of my life on earth, and all those loving years
Because you're only human, they are bound to bring you tears.
But do not be afraid to cry; it does relieve the pain.
Remember there would be no flowers unless there was some rain.
I wish that I could tell you all that God has planned
But if I were to tell you, you wouldn't understand.
But one thing is for certain, though my life on earth is o'er
I am closer to you now than I ever was before.
And to my very many friends; trust God knows what is best
I'm still not far away from you; I'm just beyond the crest.

There are rocky roads ahead of you and many hills to climb,
But together we can do it, taking one day at a time.
It was always my philosophy and I'd like it for you too,
That as you give unto the world, so the world will give to you.
If you can help somebody, who's in sorrow or pain,
Then you can say to God at night, my day was not in vain.
And now I am contented that my life it was worthwhile,
Knowing as I passed along the way, I made somebody smile.

So if you meet somebody, who is down and feeling low,
Just lend a hand to pick him up, as on your way you go.
When you are walking down the street, and you've got me on your mind,
I'm walking in your footsteps, only half a step behind.
And when you feel that gentle breeze or the wind upon your face,
That's me giving you a great big hug, or just a soft embrace.
And when it's time for you to go from that body to be free,
You're not going; you are coming here to me.
And I will always love you, from that land way up above,
We'll be in touch again soon!
PS God is sending you his love.

Author unknown

I Felt An angel

I felt an angel near today, though one I could not see
I felt an angel oh so close, sent to comfort me
I felt an angel's kiss, soft upon my cheek
And oh, without a single word of caring did it speak
I felt an angel's loving touch, soft upon my heart
And with that touch, I felt the pain and hurt within depart
I felt an angel's tepid tears, fall softly next to mine
And knew that as those tears did dry a new day would be mine
I felt an angel's silken wings enfold me with pure love
And felt a strength within me grow, a strength sent from above
I felt an angel oh so close, though one I could not see
I felt an angel near today, sent to comfort me.

Author unknown

The One I Was

I've reached my journey's end yet with a smile
And soon my shell will be but dust to dust
And though I know my going brings such grief
Mourn only for a short time if you must
But know my soul is now so full of joy
Free from the shackles of my anguished pain
My very essence in a better place
There I will bide till all shall meet again
My happy spirit soars, alive and free
I am the one I was, will always be

Pamela M Brooke

Journey's End

My love you've nearly reached your journey's end
And you may find some peace at last when there
My husband lover and my true best friend
Your suffering's been too much for you to bear
And when you leave, I know full well you must
I'll just remember all our happy days
When you were strong my love and so robust
With smiling face and all your gentle ways
I never will forget the years we had
When life stretched out with hope and future bright
Now plans we made just mock and make me sad
But oh my love, how hard you've tried to fight
You must have had in lucid moments, fears.
Yet hoping that a cure was still to be
But mostly in your long and lonely years
You did not know just who you were, or me
Now blessed peace at last my love your pain is wiped away
For yes my darling you have reached your journeys end today.

Pamela M Brooke

God's Hand

You've just walked on ahead of me
And I've got to understand
You must release the ones you love
And let go of their hand.

I try and cope the best I can
But I'm missing you so much
If I could only see you
And once more feel your touch.

Yes, you've just walked on ahead of me
Don't worry I'll be fine
But now and then I swear I feel
Your hand slip into mine.

Author unknown

Sometimes

Sometimes on our journey through life, we meet people
Who leave footprints on our mind
They challenge us to see things differently
And to question our personal reality.

Sometimes on our journey through life, we meet people
Who leave footprints on our hearts
They create a safe place for us to open our hearts
To feel loved and special.

Then sometimes on our journey through life, we meet people
Who leave footprints on our souls
They share themselves with us so profoundly that they touch
The very essence of who we are in that secret quiet place.
(Name) has left gentle footprints on the minds, hearts and
souls of many here today.
May we always remember, the beauty of her/his love
The kindness and the sacred way she/he touched our lives.

Copyright © Maggie Dent

A Loan

The Lord looked down to earth one day,
and saw a couple there.
He said, 'Now those two people make a lovely pair.
I have some spirits here with me that need a
home on earth.
I think that I shall bless these folks with a precious
spirits birth.
This baby, though, is just a loan.
These are the terms My dears,
She may live there just sixty days or she may live
for sixty years.
I hope you'll treat my spirit kindly while she's down
on earth with you.
For when she comes back here to me she has a
special job to do.

Author unknown

Tears I Cry

With flowing tears, dear cherished one,
We lay thee with the dead;
And flowers, which thou didst love so well,
Shall wave above thy head.
Sweet emblems of thy dearer self,
They find a wintry tomb;
And at the south wind's gentle touch,
Spring forth to life and bloom.
Thus, when the sun of righteousness
Shall gild thy dark abode,
Thy slumb'ring dust shall bloom afresh,
And soar to meet thy God.

Author unknown

Crossing Over

Oh, please don't feel guilty
It was just my time to go.
I see you are still feeling sad,
And the tears just seem to flow.
We all come to earth for our lifetime,
And for some it's not many years
I don't want you to keep crying
You are shedding so many tears.
I haven't really left you
Even though it may seem so.
I have just gone to my heavenly home,
And I'm closer to you than you know.

Just believe that when you say
my name, I'm standing next to you,
I know you long to see me,
But there's nothing I can do.
But I'll still send you messages
And hope you understand,
That when your time comes to
"cross over,"
I'll be there
to take your hand.

Author unknown

Passage 7   At Rest in God's Garden

As loss and grief are a part of life, at some stage someone who is beloved will die. It is something we thrust into the back of our minds, as we do not wish to deal with that hovering spectre. Inevitably that fact must indeed be faced, and a beloved appropriately farewelled to achieve a fitting closure. The celebration of the individual's life may end, but the burial will still need to be dealt with. It is when close family members and friends finally surround the sacred place where their beloved will rest. The moments are poignant and may even be upsetting. It is the ultimate 'goodbye', and an abundance of empathy is necessary. The following selection may complement these tender moments.

Requiem

Under the wide and starry sky
Dig the grave and let me lie:
Glad did I live and gladly die,
And I laid me down with a will.
This be the verse you grieve for me:
Here he lies where he longs to be;
Home is the sailor, home from the sea,
And the hunter home from the hill.

RL Stephenson

Farewell

Farewell to thee! But not farewell
To all my fondest thoughts of thee;
Within my heart they still shall dwell
And they shall cheer and comfort me.
Life seems more sweet that thou didst live
And men more true than that wert one;
Nothing is lost that thou didst give,
Nothing destroyed that thou hast done.

Anne Bronte

Some special words of comfort

The tide recedes but leaves behind
Bright seashells on the sand;
The sun goes down but gentle warmth
Still lingers on the land.
The music stops and yet
It echoes on in sweet refrain;
For every joy that passes
Something beautiful remains.
For you were a special person Jeff
Dear to our hearts
Because Jeff you were here.

Author unknown

Graveside

Do not stand at my grave and weep,
I am not there, I do not sleep.
I am in a thousand winds that blow,
I am the softly falling snow.
I am the gentle showers of rain,
I am the fields of ripening grain.
I am in the morning hush,
I am in the graceful rush
Of beautiful birds in circling flight,
I am the starshine of the night.
I am in the flowers that bloom,
I am in a quiet room.
I am in the birds that sing,
I am in each lovely thing.
Do not stand at my grave and cry,
I am not there. I do not die.

Mary Elizabeth Frye

Blessed Be

As the sun sets, so our friend has left us
As life is a day, so our friend has passed into the night
As all that falls shall rise again, so our friend will be reborn
As the Earth forms us
So our friend shall return to the Goddess and be born anew.

I call upon the Earth Mother and All Father in this time of change.
Hear these four charges and grant them with your grace.
I ask the Wind to carry her/his spirit gently towards her/his rebirth
I ask the Fire to light her/his way in her journey.
I call upon Water to ensure her/his thirst is quenched
And I ask Earth to welcome (Name) back into its embrace.

Journey on now (Name).
We will follow when we can.
May you be born again at the same time and in the same place as those you knew
and loved in this life.
May you know them again and love them again.
We will surely know you and love you for eternity.
Blessed Be.

Author unknown

God's Garden

God looked around his garden
And found an empty place;
He then looked down upon the earth
And saw your tired face.
He put his arms around you
And lifted you to rest.
God's garden must be beautiful
He always takes the best.
He knew that you were suffering
He knew you were in pain.
He knew that you would never
Get well on earth again.
He saw the road was getting rough
And the hills were hard to climb.
So he closed your weary eyelids
And whispered, 'Peace be Thine.'
It broke our hearts to lose you
But you didn't go alone,
For part of us went with you
The day God called you home.

Author unknown

Passage 8 Treasured Memories

Remembering the beloved, recalling all the treasured memories and providing them in sequential order during a farewell ceremony are important. Enhancing your delivery with the inclusion of meaningful verses, not only compensates for the colossal loss, but additionally provides words or text that may linger on in the hearts and minds of the bereaved. Finding the perfect verse is often difficult; I therefore trust this selection may contribute to a worthy recognition of the individual at the time.

Readings and Poems prior to the Pre-committal and after the Eulogy

True Love

You gave us your love and a reason to live.
You've been our best friend for so many years.
We've shared happy times and also our tears.
There's no one that means as much as you do.
After all you've done for us
And all we've been through together
So we'll never be parted it just cannot be.
For you know we love you
And we know you love us.
For as long as we can dream
For as long as we can think
As long as we have memory
We will think of you (Name).
For as long as we have eyes to see
Ears to hear, and lips to speak,
We will speak of you (Name).
As long as we have a heart to feel
A soul stirring within us
An imagination to hold you
We will remember you (Name).
As long as there is time
As long as there is love
As long as we have breath to speak your name
We will love you always and forever (Name)!

Barry H Young

A beautiful and meaningful reading applicable to a beautiful person

Footprints

One night I had a dream. I dreamed I was walking along a beach with the Lord
And across the sky flashed two sets of footprints in the sand.
One belonged to me and the other to the Lord.
When the last scene of my life flashed before me,
I looked back at the footprints in the sand.
I noticed that many times along the path of my life.
There was only one set of footprints.
I also noticed that it happened at the very lowest and saddest times in my life.
This really bothered me and I questioned the Lord about it.
'Lord, you said that once I decided to follow you,
You would walk with me all the way.
But I have noticed that during the most concerned times in my life there is only one set of footprints.
I don't understand why in times when I needed you most, you should leave me?'
The Lord replied, 'My precious I love you and I would never, never leave you
During your times of trial, tribulation and suffering when you saw only one set of footprints —
It was then I carried you!'

Author unknown

Remember Me

To the living — I am gone
To the sorrowful — I will return
To the angry, I was cheated
To the happy I am peace
To the faithful I have never left
I cannot speak, but I can listen
I cannot be seen, but I can be heard
So as you stand upon a shore gazing at a beautiful sea
As you look upon a flower and admire its simplicity
Remember me
Remember me in your heart
Your thoughts and memories
Of the times we loved, the times we cried
The times we fought, the times we laughed
And if you always think of me
I will never have gone

From Poetic Expressions *'Word of Comfort'*.
Author unknown

Memories of You

I remember everything about you,
your voice, your smile, your touch,
the way you walked, the way you talked,
the way you looked at me, meant so much.
I remember all the words you said to me,
some funny, some kind, some wise,
all of the things you did for me,
I see now with different eyes.
I remember every moment we shared,
seems like only yesterday,
or maybe it was eons ago,
It's really hard to say.
You are gone from me now,
but one thing they can't take away,
your memory resides inside my heart,
and lights up my darkest days.

Author unknown

I Had a Dream

I had a dream
I dreamt I left you
I went to a beautiful place
Where day was night and night was day
Where there were no days, no hours and no minutes
For time stood still
And all around were beautiful flowers, healing warmth and magic rainbows
With beauty around me
A winding path reached out before me
And there beckoning me were my loved ones
Those sacred and friends who had gone before me
We embraced, kissed, sang and rejoiced
My eyes were strangely dry
I was to learn that this place sheds no tears
And then I thought of you
Your hurt, your sorrow
Today so sad for me
So I ask of you
Tomorrow smile for me
Think of me with gladness
For my strength is your strength
My peace is your peace
I have never left you
And you will never leave me
Until we meet again then
But not before you're ready
I'll be waiting for you
Look for me
On a winding path that has no end

Barry H Young

Deep Peace

Deep peace of the running wave to you,
Deep peace of the flowing air to you,
Deep peace of the quiet earth to you,
Deep peace of the shining stars to you,
Deep peace of the gentle night to you,
Moon and stars pour their healing light on you,
Deep peace to you,
Blessed be.

Copyright © Wendy Haynes

A beautiful reading for a lovely woman

Imagine

If you love me
Then know that our love is eternal
That the bond we share together
Will go on forever
Imagine that I am staying with you
For a while in time
And I leave you to go into the next room.
Imagine that the room I have entered
Is filled with joy and peace and love,
Of old friends and loved ones who are delighted to see me,
Of beautiful flowers and healing warmth,
And magic rainbow colours.
Imagine how happy I will be
In that magnificent room
Now one day you will come into that room
And you will see me more beautiful and happier
Than you have ever seen me before
You will feel the same peace and joy
That I am feeling
Now if you can imagine this,
Then you will understand
That death is not an ending
But merely a passing from one room to another
In the mansions of time
For life goes on forever and love will never end.

Yvonne Goddard
A special reading that can be used for a man is 'The Dash' written
by Linda Ellis which can be found at www.lindsdlyrics.com/
thedashpoem.htm/

Words of comfort

Death Is Nothing at All

Death is nothing at all
I have slipped away into the next room
Whatever we were to each other that we are still
Call me by my old familiar name; speak to me in the easy way which we always used
Put no difference in your tone; wear no forced air of solemnity or sorrow
Laugh as we always laughed at the little jokes we enjoyed together
Play, smile, think of me; let my name be ever the household word that it always was
Let it be spoken without effort, without the ghost of a shadow on it
Life means all that it ever meant; it is the same as it ever was; there is absolute unbroken continuity
Why should I be out of mind because I am out of sight?
I am waiting for you, for an interval, somewhere very near, just around the corner
All is well.

Canon Henry Scott Holland

When someone we love dies we are faced with trying to understand one of life's great mysteries.

But I believe the following words are a way of looking at death that is comforting and makes it just a little easier to understand.

Think of me as one at rest for me you should not weep.
I have no pain, no troubled thoughts for I am just asleep
The living thinking me that was is now forever still
And life goes on without me, as time forever will.
If your heart is heavy now because I've gone away
Dwell not long upon it for none of us can stay.
Those of you who liked me I sincerely thank you all
And those of you who loved me I thank you most of all.

The answer to life's riddle I never knew
I go with hope that now I will and even so will you.
Oh, foolish, foolish me that was, I who was so small
To have wondered, even worried at the mystery of it all
And in my fleeting lifespan as time went rushing by
I found some time to hesitate
To laugh — to love — to cry
Matters it now if time began if time will ever cease

Author unknown

Passage 9   Until We Meet Again

Pre-committal

The Committal is usually one of the most difficult and painful segments within a ceremony. Not only is it the final severance, but an acknowledgment that the deceased is about to exit into the next part of his/her journey on earth. When contemplating death, one must accept that eyes that once sparkled will no longer shine, a voice once loved, will be unheard, laughter will no longer break the silence. Death is a great leveller, as it casts away barriers of creed, race, social hierarchy or appearance. In death, the deceased is in every aspect or perspective, just another life, another existence. Yet to the family, the individual has form, personality and a sense of belonging. Much empathy and discernment is called for on the part of the celebrant, who needs to diplomatically and cautiously lead a somewhat confused and stupefied gathering into an appropriate conclusion. It is hence recommended that a meaningful Verse or Reading may graciously ease and lead the gathering into the impending farewell. I refer to this as a Pre-committal for it softens the most painful part of the service.

Farewell My Friends

It was beautiful
as long as it lasted
the journey of my life.
I have no regrets whatsoever save
the pain I'll leave behind.
Those dear hearts
who love and care
and the heavy with sleep
ever moist eyes.
The smile, in spite of a
lump in the throat
and the strings pulling
at the heart and soul.
The strong arms
that held me up
when my own strength
let me down.
Each morsel that I was
fed with was full of love divine.
At every turning of my life
I came across good friends.
Friends who stood by me
even when time raced by.
Farewell, farewell
my friends.
I smile and bid you goodbye.
No, shed no tears,
for I need them not
All I need is your smile.
If you feel sad
think of me

for that's what I'd like.
When you live in the hearts
of those you love,
remember then ...
you never die.

Rabindranath Tagore

A Song of Living

Because I have loved life, I shall have no sorrow to die
I have sent up my gladness on wings, to be lost in the blue of the sky
I have run and leaped with the rain, I have taken the wind to my breast
My cheek like a drowsy child to the face of the earth I have pressed
Because I have loved life, I shall have no sorrow to die.

I have kissed young love on the lips, I have heard his song to the end
I have struck my hand like a seal in the loyal hand of a friend
I have known the peace of heaven, the comfort of work done well
I have longed for death in the darkness and risen alive out of hell
Because I have loved life, I shall have no sorrow to die.

I give a share of my soul to the world where my course is run
I know that another shall finish the task I must leave undone
I know that no flower, no flint was in vain on the path I trod
As one looks on a face through a window, through life I have looked on God
Because I have loved life, I shall have no sorrow to die.

Amelia Josephine Burr

Miss Me, but Let Me Go

Miss me, but let me go
When I come to the end of the road
And the sun has set for me
I want no rites in a gloom-filled room
Why cry for a soul set free
Miss me a little — but not too long
And not with your head bowed low
Remember the love that we once shared
Miss me — but let me go
For this is a journey that we must all take
And each must go alone
It's all a part of the Master's plan
A step on the road to home
When you are lonely, and sick of heart
Go to the friends we know
And bury your sorrows in doing good deeds
Miss me — but let me go

Author unknown

Some words of comfort

Her Journey's Just Begun

Don't think of her as gone away —
her journey's just begun,
life holds so many facets —
this earth is only one.

Just think of her as resting
from the sorrows and the tears
in a place of warmth and comfort
where there are no days and years.

Think how she must be wishing
that we could know today
how nothing but our sadness
can really pass away.

And think of her as living
in the hearts of those she touched...
for nothing loved is ever lost —
and she was loved so much.

E. Brenneman

When I Am Gone, Release Me; Let Me Go

When I am gone, release me; let me go
I have so many things to see and do.
You must not tie yourself to me with tears
Be happy that we had so many years
I gave you love; you can only guess
how much you gave me in happiness
I thank you for the love each has shown
but now it is time I travelled alone.
So grieve awhile for me if grieve you must
then let your grief be comforted by trust
It is only for a while that we must part
so bless those memories within your heart
I will not be far away, for life goes on
so if you need me, call and I will come
Though you cannot see or touch me, I will be near
and if you listen with your heart, you will hear
all of my love around you, soft and clear
Then when you must come this way alone
I will greet you with a smile and a welcome home

Author unknown

Her/his Role Down Here is Done

Her/his loving soul has touched us all
She/he didn't need to stay
Her/his spirit touched each of us
Before it sailed away
We all know souls arrive on earth
With special roles to fill
And hers/his has fully played its part
Her/his memory guides us still
She/he had a very special soul
She/he stayed for just a while
So if, or when, you're feeling sad
Recall her/him with a smile
For then you'll know inside your heart
The reason why she's/he's gone
And never feel too empty that
Her/his role down here is done
Her/his spirit touched each one of us
No other ever could
Forever we will cherish her/him
The way we know we should

Author unknown

Until We Meet Again

Each morning when we awake
we know that you are gone.
And no one knows the heartache
As we try to carry on.
Our hearts still ache with sadness
and many tears still flow.
What it meant to lose you,
No one will ever know.
Our thoughts are always with you,
your place no one can fill.
In life we loved you dearly,
In death we love you still.
There will always be a heartache,
and often a silent tear,
But always a precious memory
Of the days when you were here.
If tears could make a staircase,
And heartaches make a lane,
We'd walk the path to heaven
And bring you home again.
We hold you close within our hearts,
And there you will remain,
To walk with us throughout our lives
Until we meet again.
Our family chain is broken now,
And nothing will be the same,
But as God calls us one by one,
The chain will link again.

Author unknown

Some final words from Fred to you his family and you his friends

Some words of comfort

When I must leave you for a little while
Please do not grieve and shed with tears
And hug your sorrow to you through the years
But start out bravely with a gallant smile
And for my sake and in my name
Live on and do all the things the same
Feed not your grief on empty days
But fill each waking hour in useful ways
Reach out your hand in comfort and in cheer
And I in turn will comfort you and hold you near
'Tis only for a while that we must part
So bless those memories that lie within your heart

Author unknown

More words of comfort

You can shed tears that Jason is gone
Or you can smile because he has lived
You can close your eyes and pray that he'll come back.
Or you can open your eyes and see all he's left.
Your heart can be empty because you can't see him.
Or you can be full of love you shared.
You can turn your back on tomorrow and live yesterday.
Or you can be happy for tomorrow because of yesterday.
You can remember Jason and only that he's gone.
Or you can cherish his memory and let it live on.
You can cry and close your mind, be empty and turn your back.
Or you can do what Jason would want, smile, be happy, open your eyes, love, have fun, live and go on.

Charles Henry Bent

Some very beautiful words written countless years ago about grief

Let Me Come In

Let me come into your lives, into your hearts and share your grief whether you are
family or friend and let me take your hand in mine.
For I who have known a sorrow such as yours can understand
Let me come in — I would be very still beside you in your grief
Let me come in — I would only breathe a prayer and hold your hand.
For I have known sorrow such as yours and understand
Let me come in.

Grace Noll Crowell

Now Is the Hour

Now is the hour, to take me to my rest
With friends and family, I have been so blessed
I have loved life, so do not mourn for me
I go now down the road of memory

Think of me kindly, in all the years ahead
With love and smiles, and ne'er a tear be shed
With all my loved ones, oh how my life's been blessed
Now with glad hearts, please take me to my rest

Author unknown

Some beautiful thoughts that make death a little easier to understand

Should I Go First

Should I go first and you remain
To walk the road alone
Then live in memory's garden
With happy days we've known
In spring you'll wait for roses red
And when faded come lilacs blue
In early autumn as brown leaves fall
Of me you'll catch a glimpse or two

Should I go first and you remain
With life's battles to be fought
Every place we've visited along the way
Will be a hallowed spot
You'll hear my voice, you'll see my smile
If with your heart you listen and see
The memory of my helping hand
Will bring your thoughts of me

Should I go first and you remain
To write the next chapter alone
Let no lengthening shadows creep in
To darken the pages or the memories of our time
We've known so much happiness
We've had our cup of joy
And memory is one gift of life
That death cannot destroy.

Author unknown

One So Beloved

Through anguished, tear-filled years, love remains
And memories rustle the pages of one sweet life
The unanswered 'whys?' that were uttered
In frustrated plea, so frequently
Whilst loving hearts perceived that he was special
His life had cruel limitations.
In a kaleidoscope of pills and potions he manifested
Light and dark, fire and spirit, understanding, ambition
Persuasion and perseverance
Acknowledging neither defeat nor self-pity
Steadfastly pursuing excellence
His youth disappearing in molten dreams
'twixt days awash with tears and silent pain
An odyssey of pierced veins and bruised seams
Yet his smiles belied the turbulence
Though small, he stood so very tall with countenance
That masked a tortured spirit
Thus bravely, loving expansively, 'midst the miasma
Of drips and drugs and alien hospice
He clung to hope, though his stay on earth was done
And peace — his rightful due.
A camouflage of mindless hours and anguished minutes
Once fettered, springing free, as patterned lives
Move on — another page is turned
Come one, come all — kiss all strife goodbye and smile
For having known him!

In Leaving You Behind

Perhaps with time, this painful state fades softly from your mind
I hope and pray a piece of me, I'll quietly leave behind
My words, my actions, my spirit — the good I gently sieved
From the patterned lace of life, the tapestry I weaved.
Each tiny stitch as years passed by, bravely etched in gold
To fulfill dreams that I perceived, though buffeted and cold
The purpose of my life was real, each passing day and week
I often tried, but sometimes failed, the objectives I did seek.

If one day remembering, you hold my photo in your hand
A day when memories wash around, like waves upon the sand
Please forgive the things I said, in thoughtless frame of mind
Those wasted days, or hasty words, forgetfulness do find
For the happiness I searched in life, some joke, a song or rhyme
The bliss when targets were achieved, through dilemmas of time
The scars, the scrapes, the knocks and breaks, my soul did freely fend
I hope at last a peaceful shore is awaiting me round the bend.

Goodbye my precious loved ones
I thank you for having spent some special time with me ...

Passage of Time

Sadness passes with time
A hollow field blanketed with snow
Soon fills with swaying blooms
A darkened sky suddenly illuminates
A weary traveller's way
And Spring follows a Winter's road
Which butterflies array
Somewhere, somehow, shadows
Give way to sunbeams
Life's fabric is painted with promised purpose
And each day, new freshness springs
Laughter envelops an empty room
And a broken heart sings
With an abandonment of joy
As it finally kisses the dawn
Of a bright new day!

Cry Not for Me ...

Shadows fall upon the world of my loved ones
They no longer see the dew upon the rose
The sun has slipped behind a darkened rain cloud
Their souls are clenched in pain as sorrow grows
From the surface of their minds they have set forth
Pursuing each daily chore with melancholy face
That yields no more, no less than asked
And yet, I long to reach right out and say aloud
Cry not for me my friends; hear the music in my heart
And kiss my memory — 'Farewell'

I have lived so well upon this earth
I have followed many paths to reach the sun
If I had troubles, or pain, or heartaches
I cherished more the smiles, a thousand more, when one
Had said to me in friendship — 'I wish you well!'
They were sweet words I treasured long.
To the hilltops, to the clouds to the moon and stars beyond
To a pasture glistening with fresh rain — I run
So, cry not for me, my friends, hear the music in my heart
And kiss my memory 'Farewell'

Let Me Go

I have got to leave you, bid me farewell, my friends, my family
I bow to you all and take my departure
I have come to the end of the road
And the sun has set for me
I want no tears in a gloom filled room
Why cry for a soul set free
For to live in the hearts of those we love is not to die
Miss me — but let me go
Miss me a little — but not for long
And not with your head bowed low
Remember the joy and love that once was shared
Memory is the treasury and keeper of all things
Miss me — but let me go
For this is a journey we must all take
A summons has come and I am ready for the journey
As each must go alone
Miss me — but let me go

Author unknown

Heaven's Stairs

The day I died was just an ordinary day, sunny beautiful and calm, the only
difference was I saw heaven's stairs and the good Lord's holy palm
I felt relieved and at peace, I saw this glorious stone staircase over an ocean
With colorful flowers on the sides
I knew that I wouldn't have to worry; I knew that God
would be there for me. I saw those who had gone before me, smiling ever so bright
in this happy home they call 'heaven'
The Lord even came to meet me, so graceful, strong and tall

He called me home to paradise; he took me from it all
I started my way up to heaven; I climbed stair by stair
I knew it would be worth it, because at the top God waited there
I knew that those who grieved knew body-wise I was gone
But in each and every one of them, my spirit lived on and on
He said your life is over, new life would be grasped
And that my memory would live on forever, even though I'd passed

Domenic Vincenzo Ferrari

Passage 10 At Peace and At Rest

The Committal

The committal is an extremely heart-wrenching part of a funeral service. It is an extremely difficult time for the family and friends of the deceased person. In contemplating death, we understand life. Death softens any hardened heart, connects the immediate family, and draws those who have drifted apart for years, in a gentle embrace of supportiveness during grief. It is therefore most important for the celebrant to select the perfect passage that will leave the gathering with a sense of peace, togetherness and closure. The following are passages applicable to non-religious or religious funeral services.

Would you please be upstanding?

Tenderly and reverently we commit the body of Helen to the ground
We are grateful for the life that has been lived
And for all that life has meant to us
We are glad Helen lived.
We are glad we saw her face and felt the pressure of her hand
We cherish the memories of her words, her warmth, her deeds, her character and her friendship
And most of all we cherish her love.

Copyright © Dally Messenger

Would you please be upstanding?

We honour the life of (Name)
And the love that he has brought into our lives.
We say farewell (Name)
May we leave this space with a call for peace and compassion.
May we embrace the grief and grow through it.
Many blessings and gratitude, may peace be with you.

Copyright © Wendy Haynes

Committal reading

As we say farewell to (Name) let us hear words by Dorothy McRae-McMahon on the thoughts of the Buddha

The first truth is that nothing is lost in the universe
Matter turns into energy
Energy turns into matter
A dead leaf turns into soil
A seed sprouts and becomes a new plant
Old solar systems disintegrate and turn into cosmic rays
We are born of our parents; our children are born of us
Let us now meditate on beauty of the bush and nature that (Name) so loved
Our thoughts can be a message of the love we have for (Name)
And for this earth and its wonders.
May the gentle rain visit our earth with its greening of life
May the winds of freedom move in delight among the trees
And connect its breathing and growing with the spirit of (Name)
May the sun light it and warm it with love every day
Just as we have loved (Name)
And as he has loved us
Let us go in peace.

Dorothy McRae-McMahon

Committals with a religious theme

It is now time to say goodbye to (Name). There is sadness in his passing but we take comfort in the hope that one day we shall see him again. Although this congregation will disperse in sorrow, the mercy of God will gather us together again in the joy of his kingdom.

Please be upstanding 1

May eternal rest be granted unto (Name) O Lord, and let perpetual light shine upon him.

    Tenderly and reverently, we will commit the body of (Name) to the purifying elements, grateful for the life that has been lived and for all that life has meant to us.

    We now leave (Name) in peace. With much love and respect we bid him fare-well. Thus in thinking of (Name) , let us leave this place in quietness of spirit and live with concern and affection for one another.

Please be upstanding 2

Let us commend (Name) into the hands of God, our Maker and Redeemer.

    O God our heavenly Father, who by Thy mighty power has given us life, and by Thy loving kindness has bestowed upon us new life in Jesus Christ. We commend to Thy merciful keeping Thy servant (Name) , our loved one here departed.

    Take (Name) into the love and safety of Thy everlasting comfort.

    Through Jesus Christ, Thy son of God

    Who died and rose again to save us.

    Amen

Passage 11 Thy Will Be Done

The Benediction

I strongly recommend a benediction at the conclusion of a ceremony, to provide a sense of peace and hope. Hope for the future, hope to heal wounds, hope that relationships may be improved, familial breakdowns repaired. Frequently, the harshness of death awakens realities and new perspectives. Further, an untimely death aids some individuals to take stock and readjust their own lives before it is too late. Words are particularly comforting and provide the bereaved with the will to move on, live life to its fullest and believe that every living moment should be captured, held tight in one's heart and lovingly cherished. The following benedictions are non-religious as well as religious.

For a non-religious service

We now leave the memory of our beloved Helen in peace
With enduring love and respect we wish her farewell
May you all find richness and example in your many memories of Helen
May you find strength and support in your love for one another and may you find
peace in your hearts

If there are many young people in the congregation — sons,
daughters, grandchildren — then can add

There are many young people here today so let us promise Cliff to have a devotion
to all things worthwhile and make our lives meaningful and of worth.

For non-religious or religious service

The act is done. The words have been said.
The gate of the coming hour now opens to us in peace.
Let us go through with thanksgiving for all that we said and did in this hour
Blessed is the mystery of life and death, which is our own
And blessed be love forever.
Amen

Copyright © Sarah York (Remembering Well)

Religious Benedictions

May the Lord bless us and keep us, may the Lord make his face shine upon us, and be gracious unto us, and may the Lord lift up His countenance upon us
   Amen

Or

The grace of the Lord Jesus Christ and the love of God, and the fellowship of the Holy Spirit, be with us all evermore
   Amen

Or

The Lord bless you and keep you
The Lord make his face to shine upon you, and be gracious to you
The Lord lift up his countenance upon you
And give you peace
Amen

Or

Peace be to us all, and love with faith
From God the Father and the Lord Jesus Christ
Amen

Or

Now to him who is able to keep us from falling, and to present us faultless before the presence of his glory with everlasting joy, to the only wise God our Saviour, be glory and majesty, dominion and power, both now and ever

   Amen

A lovely ending to a funeral service

The warmth of her love
May you always feel it
The sparkle of her Spiritedness
May you always sense it
The music in her laughter
May you always hear it
The strength of her footprints
May you wisely follow
The life she designed
May her artistry move you
And may the impressions she made
Be mirrored by you!

Copyright © Ruth Van Gramberg

Passage 12 The Long Day Closes

Occasionally, a family may request the celebrant to conduct a ceremony for the internment of ashes in a cemetery or any other carefully selected sacred place. This is very personal and forms part of the grieving process. The deceased may have made this decision prior to his demise, or the family may have decided what they believed to be the perfect conclusion. This personal preference should therefore be evaluated and arranged with compassion and understanding. Carefully worded verses will enable this beautiful ritual to be handled with dignity. I trust the following may assist in your deliberations.

Ashes to Ashes — Dust to Dust

In placing the ashes of May in this hallowed ground,
We recall once more, all that our loved May has meant to us.
We dedicate this simple plot, amid these natural surroundings,
To every beautiful and precious memory associated with her.
We lay these ashes in that gentle earth which has been the chief support of man.
Since first he walked beneath the sun from which all life comes and to which all life
in the end returns.
To all human beings, to all living forms, the soil has ever provided the sustenance
that is the staff of life.
To that good earth we now commit the ashes of May and we are grateful for the
life that has been lived
And for all that life has meant to us.
We are glad May lived.
We are glad we saw her face and felt the pressure of her hand.
We cherish the memories of her words, her deeds and her lovely character.
We cherish her friendship. But most of all we cherish her love.
May you find strength, support in your love for one another and may you find
peace in your hearts.
Let us now leave this sacred place in quietness of spirit and live with care, love and
concern for one another.

Adapted from anonymous readings by Barry H Young

Or

In placing the ashes of Rueben in this hallowed ground, we think again of all that our loved companion and friend meant and means to us. Thus we dedicate this plot, amid these natural surroundings, to every beautiful and precious memory associated with her.

We lay these ashes in this gentle earth which has been the chief support of Man since first he walked beneath the sun. To all human beings, to all living forms, the soil has ever provided the sustenance that is the staff of life. To that good earth we now commit the ashes of our beloved Rueben.

> *Ashes to ashes*
> *Dust to dust*
> *We commit the body of our beloved Rueben*

Adapted from anonymous readings by Barry H Young

Or

Ashes to ashes
Dust to dust
Memory to memory
Story to story
Blessing to blessing
Strength to strength
Spirit to spirit
Love to love.
We commit the body of Barbara

Copyright © Sarah York (Remembering Well)

Passage 13 Let Us Pray

Religion plays an important role in many people's lives and religious ceremonies or rituals are traditionally part of marking life's most important milestones. Our flexibility as celebrants allows us to include religious aspects within a service. This willingness enables the family to feel confident that the celebrant will abide by their wishes and respectfully present the selected text or verses. It is most important to proclaim and extend this availability and amenable attitude at the inception of the interview process. It is the family who is important; it is the family's request and therefore it is the celebrant's duty to willingly comply and restore their faith and trust in God to heal their hearts and thus move on.

A Prayer for the One Who Is Left

*Lord, the trouble about life just now
is that I seem to have all things
which don't matter, and to have
lost all the things that do matter.*

*I have life
I have enough money to occupy me
but I am alone
and sometimes I feel that
nothing can make up for that.*

*Lord compel me to see
the meaning of my faith
Make me realise
that I have hope
as well as a memory, and
the unseen cloud of witness
is around me
That you meant it when
You said that You would
always be with me.*

*And make me realise that
as long as You leave me here
there is something that
I am meant to do
and in doing it, help me
to find the comfort and the
courage that I need to go on
Amen.*

Author unknown

Parental Prayer ...
From a Loving Mother

Do not resent me for the discipline and guidance
I handed out with 'double servings'
Do not condemn me for the mistakes I made —
As I had no prior rehearsals.
Do not judge me harshly — for you may
One day, duplicate my shadow
As when I no longer live and am
But an image — dusty on a shelf
And the word 'Mum' is spoken of as 'Nan'
Just remember —
I gave you life
I learned many things with you,
As I was still a child myself.
I learned to love and understand
As pain, anxiety, happiness and sorrow
Combined as my only tutor
And I found laughter with you and
For you, as you were but an
Extension of myself —
And but a link with all your tomorrows!

Let Us Pray 1

May peace soothe your heart and mind,
May grace lift up your eyes to the gifts that are present in all things.
You come this day with reverent hearts,
You bring your grief and your gratitude,
Your acceptance and your confusion.
In your heartache you are not alone,
Knowing that we all have to live with questions unanswered,
We are set free when we face our sorrow and our loss.
There is courage and strength in light of the fear,
Revealed when we are still.
In the shared space of respect and care, all is welcome,
Love, grace and peace always present,
As we grieve and as we laugh.
In this sharing may our distress be eased and may we feel comforted.
Amen

Copyright © Wendy Haynes

Let Us Pray 2

Eternal Father.
God of all consolation.
In Your unending love and mercy for us.
You turn the darkness of death into the dawn of new life.
Be our refuge and strength in sorrow.
We ask that You take (Name) into your fold.
For as Your son, our Lord Jesus Christ.
By dying for us conquered death.
And by rising restored us to life.
So may we go forward in faith to meet Him.
And after our life on earth.
We ask this through Jesus Christ our Lord.
Amen.

Let us now take a moment to prayerfully reflect on Bob's life journey and to remember those who need our support at this time

We are thankful for the gift of Bob's life; a life lived with love and dedicated to the nurture of his family.

Bob, you will always be part of our spirit, always carried tenderly beneath the heart; a saving memory of closeness and gifts given.

Even as we grieve this loss let us commit ourselves to the comfort of those who will miss Bob most, especially his beloved wife Shirl.

Let us surround her with our love and comfort.

There will be times when pain and fatigue are our companions,

In these times let there be room in our hearts for strength.

There will be days and nights filled with darkness,

In those times may the light of courage find its place.

Help us to endure the suffering and dissolve the fear.

Renew within us the calm spirit of trust and peace.

Let us go into the world glad that we have loved Bob, free to weep for the one we have lost but empowered to live life to the full, as he did.

We trust that Bob will find that place within creation where great happiness, contentment and peace will be his.

May his love and life stay all the more with us now that he has left us.

And may our love for him now give us the strength to continue to show our love and support for each other as we travel the road without Bob at our side.

Amen

Let us now take a moment to prayerfully reflect on Allison's life journey and to remember those who need our support at this time

We are thankful for the gift of Allison's life, a life lived with love and dedicated to others.
We will imagine our love soaring high, spreading wide, surrounding Allison in any place.
There is no place where our love will not reach her.
No time when we will forget her.
Allison, you will always be part of our spirit always carried tenderly beneath the heart; a saving memory of closeness and gifts given.
Even as we grieve this loss let us commit ourselves to the comfort of those who will miss Allison most, especially Noel.
Let us surround him with our love and comfort.
There will be times when pain and fatigue are our companions.
In these times let there be room in our hearts for strength.
There will be days and nights filled with darkness.
In those times, may the light of courage find its place.
Help us to endure the suffering and dissolve the fear.
Renew within us the calm spirit of trust and peace.
Let us go into the world glad that we have loved Allison, free to weep for the one we have lost but empowered to live life to the full.
We trust that Allison will find that place within creation where great happiness, contentment and peace will be hers.
May her love and life stay all the more with us now that she has left us.
And may our love for her now give us the strength to continue to show our love and support for each other as we travel the road without Allison at our side.
Amen

Let Us Pray

Eternal God, you have shared with us the life of Hugh.

Before he was ours, he was yours. For all that Hugh has given us to make us what we are, for that of him which lives and grows in each of us, and for his life that in your love will never end, we give you thanks.

You have cared for him while he lived upon this earth and we know you will continue to care for him from this day forward.

While we are uncertain about the future, we know we are always in your loving hands and when in your hands all will be well.

Thank you for the life you gave us in the person of Hugh.

As now we offer Hugh back into your arms, comfort us in our loneliness, strengthen us in our weakness, and give us courage to face the future, O Divine Master.

Grant that I may not so much seek to be consoled as to console;

To be understood, as to understand, unafraid.

Draw those of us who remain in this life closer to one another, make us faithful to serve one another, and give us to know peace and joy

May we be assured of the life that continues after this life on earth and be comforted knowing that this is not the end of all of life but a beginning of a new life. We ask this prayer in Jesus' name.

Amen.

This is a suitable prayer that can be used on almost every occasion

Eternal Father, God of all consolation.

In your unending love and mercy for us.

You turn the darkness of death into the dawn of life.

Be our refuge and strength in sorrow. We ask that You take (Name) into your fold.

For as Your son, our Lord Jesus Christ, by dying for us conquered death

And by rising restored us to life

So may we go forward in faith to meet him, and after our life on earth.

We ask this through Jesus Christ our Lord.

Amen

Let Us Pray

God our Father
Uphold us by Your Spirit
Enable us to show Your compassion
Give us in our sorrow the calm of Your peace
May our grief give way to joy
Through Jesus Christ our Lord
Amen

O Divine Master

Grant that I may not so much seek to be consoled as to console;
To be understood, as to understand;
To be loved, as to love;
For it is in giving that we receive;
It is in pardoning that we are pardoned
And it is in dying that we are born to Eternal Life.
Amen

Indian Prayer

When I am dead
Cry me a little
Think of me sometimes
But not too much
Think of me now and again
As I was in life
At some moments it's pleasant to recall
But not for long
Leave me in peace
And while you live
Let your thoughts be with the living

Author unknown

Irish Blessing

May the road rise to meet you
May the wind be always at your back
May the sun shine upon your face
The rains fall softly upon the fields
And until we meet again, may you be held in the palm of God's hand.
Amen

A beautiful prayer read out at a police officer's funeral service and sometimes used in ceremonial functions

The Police Prayer

God, we know it is from you that we have learned what goodness and justice are.
You have given members of the New South Wales Police Service the task of maintaining law and order in the community.
We seek the strength to meet the many challenges encountered in this endeavour.
Give us the courage and the resolution to do our duty at all times, and such a respect and love for justice, that neither promise nor threat, will ever make us depart from it.
Enable us, by your presence, to be protector of the endangered, friend to all, and role model to the children and youth of the community, when called upon to be adviser, may we be inspired with your wisdom and truth.
Grant us the skill and wisdom we need to triumph over wrong, in our role of protecting the community.
Guide us when to enforce, and when to relax the letter of the law. Help us to be perfect examples of the honesty, the goodness, and the justice which is our duty to maintain, and grant that our actions will inspire in our community, confidence in its police officers.
We make our prayer through you, the one true life affirming God.
Amen

Reverend Barry May

A Prayer for Bereavement

Father, eyes blinded by the symbols of sorrow cannot see the stars. I, at this moment, can see nothing beyond my own grief. I have been face to face with misery and loneliness in these days; with the strangeness of life and death that takes away a loved one and gives no explanation; with the mystery of Providence I have tried to understand and cannot understand.

Thou, Holy Spirit, Thou visitor is sorrow. Thou who art acquainted with human tears and broken hearts, sorely I need Thy help now.

Because my heart is sore, I have shut the door of my heart to my fellows, even to Thee. But I sense that withdrawal and the effort to dull my feelings is not the way toward healing. Help me now to dare to my being wide to the balm of Thy loving Spirit, unafraid of any depth of height or intensity of overflowing emotion.
Open.
Thou has promised to wipe away all tears from our eyes.
I ask Thee to fulfil that promise now.
Thou hast promised to bind up our wounded spirits,
I ask Thee to fulfil that promise now.
Thou hast promised to give us peace, not as the world gives but in the midst of our trouble. I ask Thee to fulfil that promise now.
Thou has promised to be with us always.
I ask Thee to fulfil that promise now
I therefore thank Thee that Thou art walking beside me every step of the way.
I put my hand in Thine, and walk on into the future, knowing that it will be a good future because Thou art in it.
Amen

Peter Marshall

A Prayer for One Who Will Not Be Comforted

Father, we join our prayers in asking Thy help for this one, who bereaved, still feels lonely. He has not even yet found the joy of Thy Resurrection and the sense of the presence of one he loves who is with Thee. Grant that we may feel her near, may somehow be persuaded that she still lives, that she is happy, that she still loves him as he loves her.

May such assurances come to all the hearts that need them today. We ask in the name of our Lord.
Amen.

Peter Marshall

The Prayer of St Francis

Lord, make us an instrument of your peace
Where there is hatred, let there be love
Where there is injury, pardon
Where there is discord, unity
Where there is doubt, faith
Where there is error, truth
Where there is despair, hope
Where there is sadness, joy
Where there is darkness, light

For those of you who wish, please join with me in saying the Lord's Prayer

Our Father, which art in Heaven
Hallowed be Thy name
Thy Kingdom come
Thy will be done, on earth
As it is in Heaven
Give us this day our daily bread
And forgive us our trespasses
As we forgive those who trespass against us
And lead us not into temptation but deliver us from evil
For Thine is the Kingdom
The power and the glory
For ever and ever
Amen

As a tribute to Helen I will now read the beautiful Psalm of strength and comfort — Psalm 23

The Lord is my shepherd: I shall not want
He maketh me to lie down in green pastures
He leadeth me beside the still waters
He restoreth my soul
He leadeth me in the paths of righteousness for his name's sake
Yea though I walk through the valley of the shadow of death, I will fear no evil
For Thou art with me, Thy rod and Thy staff they comfort me
Thou preparest a table before me in the presence of mine enemies
Thou anointest my head with oil
My cup runneth over
Surely goodness and mercy shall follow me all the days of my life
And I will dwell in the house of the Lord forever
Amen.

Reading from the Scriptures Ecclesiastes Chapter 3

To everything there is a season
To everything there is a reason
And a time for every purpose
A time to be born and a time to die
A time to weep and a time to laugh
A time to mourn and a time to dance
A time to get and a time to lose
A time to keep and a time to give away
A time of war and a time of peace
A time to be happy and a time to love

Adaptation by Barry H Young

From the Prophet

Your pain is the breaking of the shell that encloses your understanding
Even as the stone of the fruit must break, that its heart may stand in the sun,
So must you know pain.
And could you keep your heart in wonder at the daily miracles of your life,
Your pain would not seem less wondrous than your joy,
And you would accept the seasons of your heart,
Even as you have always accepted the seasons that pass over your fields,
And you would watch with serenity through the winters of your grief.

Kahlil Gibran

Prayer of Faith

We trust that beyond absence there is a presence
That beyond the pain there can be healing
That beyond the brokenness there can be wholeness
That beyond the anger there may be peace
That beyond the hurting there may be forgiveness
That beyond the silence there may be the word
That beyond the word there may be understanding
That through understanding there is love

Author unknown

Life Must Go On

Grieve for me, for I would grieve for you
Then brush away the sorrow and the tears
Life is not over, but begins anew
With courage you must greet the coming years
To live forever in the past is wrong
Can only cause you misery and pain
Dwell not on memories overlong
With others you must share and care again
Reach out and comfort those who comfort you
Recall the years, but only for a while
Nurse not your loneliness; but live again
Forget not. Remember with a smile.

Navaho Prayer

A Mother

You can only have one mother
Patient kind and true
No other friend in all the world
Will be the same to you
When other friends forsake you
To mother you will return
For all her loving kindness
She asks nothing in return
As we look upon her picture
Sweet memories we recall
Of a face so full of sunshine
And a smile for one and all
Sweet Jesus, take this message
To our dear mother up above
Tell her how we miss her
And give her all our love

Irish Funeral Prayer

Passage 14 A Bud to Bloom
in Heaven

*T*he death of a baby is a unique challenge for a funeral celebrant as the usual practice of focusing on a life lived, celebrating good times, achievements and experiences, does not apply. Instead the celebrant is faced with the challenge of creating a meaningful ritual to mark the loss of a life unlived, of special times that were never shared, and that death was either expected because of illness, or cruelly cut short. Consequently, the parent may feel lost, bewildered or distressed. A celebrant has the ability to gently persuade the family member to cope with the child's death by selecting an appropriate verse or reading, to ease the burden of grief. The presentation of a pertinent verse may also encompass and infuse the bereaved family members, with a perspective of acceptance. It may further provoke or engender a freshened spiritual belief and purpose to move forward into the future.

The following passages including prayers are examples that can be used to connect to the grieving parents and bring comfort to them

You Left without Saying Goodbye

A little child appeared one day
A little cherub sent my way
He gently touched my heart, my hand
Then swiftly flew this unknown land
It seemed so cruel, the regret is so deep
Where are you baby — can you hear me now weep
You left without saying goodbye!
Was it part of life's destiny
What is the reason — explain it to me
A shadow, a whisper, a gentle sun's ray
You lived, you breathed, then slipped far away
Your beautiful smile — it comforts each dream
It soothes my sorrow and stifles my scream
It seemed so cruel, the regret is so deep
Where are you baby — can you hear me now weep
You left without saying goodbye!
Wretched and empty, my thoughts in turmoil
Your imprint on pillow, where you lingered awhile
A finger that pointed, then slipped into mine
The more I remember, the more I pine
It seemed so cruel, the regret is so deep
Where are you baby — can you hear me now weep
You left without saying goodbye!

Goodbye Little One

My little one, you filled my world, heaven sent to me
A sunbeam in a darkened room, a gift from God to see
Your smile, so sweet and tender
You touched my very soul
You helped me grow, strong and tall
That was your little role
You had to go, your time was right, cold emptiness you leave
A life so short, so pure, so loved, hearts you touched — now grieve.

Is it some greater puzzle — I can never understand
I was a mother, parent for a while — I felt so grand
Now all that's left are memories
Framed in black and white
And this pain, deep and tearing
When you flew away from sight
But my little one, my pretty one, when I see the stars above
You will always shine the brightest in the heaven of our love.

Copyright © Ruth Van Gramberg

So Special

She was so very, very special
And was so from the start
You held her in your arms
But mainly in your heart
And like a single drop of rain
That on still waters fall,
Her life did ripples make
And touched the lives of all.
She's gone to play with angels
In heaven up above
So keep your special memories
And treasure them with love
Although your darling daughter
Was with you just a while
She'll live on in your heart
With a sweet remembered smile

Author unknown

Angels

The sky is filled with Angels
With puffy lacy wings
The remnants of God's beauty
With treasures they now bring
Each one of them a Guardian
That travels in the sky
To watch throughout eternity
Their parents from on high
Smiles that come from Angels
They fall like crystal rain
Eases earthly burdens
Lifting all life's pain
Halos so astounding
That glitter gold each day
Following their loved ones
In such a perfect way
Wings in gentle breezes
That fall from up above
Kissing every parent
With everlasting love
Angels soar through heaven
With everlasting light
Looking down from heaven
Saying their "goodnights"
Kissing all who loved them
So gently on the face
This life's tender mercy
Each parent can embrace
Wings and shiny halos
Travel from on high
Surrounding all their loved ones
They never say good-bye.

Author unknown

Snowdrops

The world may never notice
If a snowdrop doesn't bloom,
Or even pause to wonder
If the petals fall too soon.
But every life that ever forms,
Or ever comes to be,
Touches the world in some small way
For all eternity.
The little one we longed for
Was swiftly here and gone.
But the love that was then planted
Is a light that still shines on.
And though our arms are empty,
Our hearts know what to do.
Every beating of our hearts
Says that we love you.

Author unknown

We Will Meet Again

Time has taken me from you,
Although not very far.
I'll be watching through the sunshine
And through the brightest star.
I'll be watching all of you,
From the heavens up above.
So take good care of each other
And carry all my love.
If you're ever wondering
If I'm there, here's where you can start.
Take a look inside yourself
Deep within your heart.
I'll always be your baby,
Your child (grandchild) , your best friend.
So anytime you need me,
Close your eyes I'm back again.

Author unknown

Fly

Performed/recorded by Celine Dion. These words are very beautiful, moving and comforting for the funeral of a child.

A tender reading that demonstrates God's caring for precious Ethan

Child Loaned

I will lend you for a little while a child of mine, He said,
For you to love the time she lives and mourn for when she's gone.
It may be just for a very short time,
But will you, till I call her home, take care of her for me?
She'll bring her charms to gladden you and should her stay be brief
You will have her loving memories as solace for your grief.
I cannot promise she will stay, since all from earth return,
But there are lessons taught down there I want this child to learn.
I have looked this wide world over, in search of teachers true
And from the crowds that throng life's lanes
I have selected you.
Now will you give her all your love, nor think the labour vain,
Nor hate me when I come to call and take her back again?
I fancied that I heard them say,
Dear Lord, Thy will be done,
For all the joy this child shall bring, the risk of grief we'll run.
We will shelter her with tenderness and love her while we may
And for the happiness we have known, forever grateful stay.
But should we have to call her much sooner than we'd planned
We'll brave the bitter grief that comes and try to understand.

Edgar Guest

Some words of comfort

Life does proceed
When a loved one leaves
But it's difficult for us
Who are left to grieve.
We'll pick ourselves up
And try again.
We'll make the effort.
To function again.
It won't be easy
As we well know.
But we won't give up
The change made us grow.
We loved Ethan so much
And fate was unkind.
He went away first.
He left us behind.
The pain in our hearts.
Will remain yet awhile.
But yesterday's gone.
Tomorrow we'll try and smile.

Author unknown

Sleep Soft

Sleep soft dear child in Heavenly peace
as angels now surround thee
Released from mortal chains of earth
your time here was decreed.
Yet though our hearts be troubled
and cold like winter chill
The love that burned will always shine
on a destiny now fulfilled.
Ours not to ask the reason why
this hill we had to climb
As we held and touched a special gift
for just a little time.
A new star burns so brightly now
and always will be here
Within our hearts, within our souls
to chase away the tears.
We think now of the wondrous things;
the birth, the joy and love
Not given, but lent for a while
and returned to Heaven above.

John Foster

A tender reading that explains a higher meaning for precious Ethan

When God calls little children to dwell with him above, we mortals sometime question the wisdom of His love. Perhaps God tires of calling the aged to His fold, so he picks a rosebud before it can grow old. God knows how much we need them, and so he takes but few to make the land of Heaven more beautiful to view. Believing this is difficult, still somehow we must try, the saddest word mankind knows will always be 'Goodbye'. So when a little child departs we who are left behind must realise God loves children, Angels are hard to find.

Cindy O'Connor

The Angels Called

*The Angels called on Friday
And took you by the hand
And whispered, 'Jesus needs you more, in our promised land'*

Author unknown

A Loan

The Lord looked down to earth one day
and saw a couple there.
He said, 'Now those two people make a lovely pair.
I have some spirits here with Me that need a
home on earth.
I think that I shall bless these folks with a precious
spirits birth.
This baby, though, is just a Loan.
These are the terms, My dears,
She may live there just sixty days or she may live
for sixty years.
I hope you'll treat My spirit kindly while she's down
on earth with you.
For when she comes back here to Me she has a
special job to do.'

With flowing tears, dear cherished one,
We lay thee with the dead;
And flowers, which thou didst love so well,
Shall wave above thy head.
Sweet emblems of thy dearer self,
They find a wintry tomb;
And at the south wind's gentle touch,
Spring forth to life and bloom.
Thus, when the sun of righteousness
Shall gild thy dark abode,
Thy slumb'ring dust shall bloom afresh,
And soar to meet thy God.

Author unknown

A Special Reading from the Gospel of St Luke

People were bringing babies to Jesus to have him touch them.
When the disciples saw this they rebuked them.
But Jesus called the little children to him and said,
'Let the children come to me and do not hinder them for the Kingdom of God belongs to such as these'.

Another reading that could be used here is *Only as a Child* by Helen Steiner Rice from her book — *Just For You.*

Mathew 19-13-15

People brought little children to Jesus, for him to lay his hands on them and say a prayer. The disciples turned them away, but Jesus said, 'Let the children alone, and do not stop them from coming to me, for it is to such as these that the kingdom of heaven belongs.' Then he laid hands on them and went on his way. Ethan it is to you that the Kingdom of heaven belongs. May you be welcomed into heaven and be embraced by God's deep love for you.

I will now read from the scriptures the beautiful psalm of fortitude and comfort — the 23rd Psalm

Psalm 23

The Lord is my shepherd: I shall not want
He maketh me to lie down in green pastures
He leadeth me beside the still waters
He restoreth my soul
He leadeth me in the paths of righteousness for His name's sake
Yea though I walk through the valley of the shadow of death, I will fear no evil
For Thou art with me
Thy rod and Thy staff they comfort me
Thou preparest a table before me in the presence of mine enemies
Thou anointest my head with oil
My cup runneth over
Surely goodness and mercy shall follow me all the days of my life
And I will dwell in the house of the Lord forever
Amen.

Words of comfort

May your beautiful son, Ethan, come to know eternal peace and love. May grace and light be with you in your sorrow and give you healing and peace. May you continue to find strength in your loving commitment to each other. May you be held and comforted by those around you as your heart grieves. May your love for yourself and others be deepened. May you be blessed with new life.

May you know the kind, gentle embrace of God.
There were many things we wanted to give to you Ethan
There were many dreams we had for our life together with you.
All these hopes and dreams we held for you, Ethan
May the love we have for you reach out into the universe and touch your fragile spirit

Time has taken me away from you
Although not very far
I'll be watching through the sunshine
And through the brightest star
I'll be watching all of you
From the heavens up above
So take good care of each other
And carry all my love
If you're ever wondering if I'm there, here's where you start
Take a look inside yourself
Deep within your heart
I'll always be your little boy

Author unknown

For a Young Child

Time has taken me away from you
Although not very far
I'll be watching through the sunshine
And through the brightest star
I'll be watching all of you
From the heavens up above
So take good care of each other
And carry all my love
If you're ever wondering
If I'm there, here's where you start
Take a look inside yourself
Deep within your heart
I'll always be your little girl/boy
So any time you need me
Close your eyes
I'm back again

Author unknown

She Was Special

She was so very, very special
And so from the start
You held her in your arms
But mainly in your heart
And like a single drop of rain
That still waters fall
Her life did ripples make
And touched the lives of all

She's gone to play with the angels
In heaven up above
So keep your special memories
And treasure them with love

Although your darling (Name)
Was with you just a while
She'll live on in your hearts
With a sweet remembering smile

Author unknown

Sometimes, When the Sun Goes Down

Sometimes, when the sun goes down,
It seems it will never rise again...
but it will!
Sometimes, when you feel alone,
It seems your heart will break in two...
but it won't.
And sometimes, it seems
It's hardly worthwhile carrying on...
But it is.
For sometimes, when the sun goes down,
It seems it will never rise again,
But it does

Frank Brown

A Prayer

God of love and compassion we join together today in this moment to bless and
pray for this precious baby Ethan
This precious son began life with (Names of parents)
In this they are now parents and will hold Ethan in their hearts for all times.
Ethan we bless you with all our love.

With confidence and trust let us place Ethan into God's loving care.
Ethan, our love goes with you as we entrust you into God's care.
May God bless you and smile on you and grant you peace now and forever.
May the love of your parents etc. hold you gently.
Go in peace our precious child.
Amen

A Prayer

Creator and designer of the universe and nature.
We commend baby Ethan to you.
You care for little children in this present life and for them in the life to come, a
home where they behold your Father's face.
We ask only that Ethan finds another place in your creation where great
happiness will be his.
For you have said, 'Let the children come unto me, for to such belongs the
Kingdom of Heaven'.
And may our love for Ethan stay all the more with us because you have taken him.
Give us the strength to love each other more and all creation better because of Ethan.
Amen

A Prayer for the Parents

God of hope and grieving, we are silent in your presence
  Help us to know that every life is whole in your eyes, no dream incomplete in
your heart.
  Grant that we may come before you and each other with a measure of gratitude
for the gifts we have been given — for the privilege of this bitter celebration in the
circle of supportive family and friends, for the possibility of healing, for the promise
of the sunrise after the lengthy desperation of grief's night.
  Give to (Parents' Names) the courage to continue. Grant that they may hold
fast to one another in this time of sorrow and that their family and friends may find
the strength to be supportive, not backing away from the intensity of grief.

Let the stories be told over and over.
Let the tears be honoured as a token of caring and love.
Let the dreams be named and not forgotten.
Let anger be in time eased into forgiveness.

Spirit of compassion, inspire these people to hug easily and often, for it is your hand that soothes us through this human touch. Let all hopes be cherished, that they may find a new focus and in due course come to live again.

Spirit of Life and Hope, we trust that you have taken (Name)'s spirit to your bosom. Help now those who remain on this earth, those whose challenge it is to reconstruct their lives and begin again in love.

Amen

Barbara Carlson

Desiderata

Go placidly amid the noise and haste, and remember what peace there may be in silence. As far as possible without surrender be on good terms with all persons. Speak your truth quietly and clearly and listen to others, even the dull and ignorant; they too have their story.

Avoid loud and aggressive persons; they are vexations to the spirit. If you compare yourself with others, you may become vain and bitter, for always there will be greater and lesser persons than yourself. Enjoy your achievements as well as your plans.

Keep interested in your own career, however humble; it is a real possession in the changing fortunes of time. Exercise caution in your business affairs, for the world is full of trickery. But let this not blind you to what virtue there is; many persons strive for high ideals, and everywhere life is full of heroism.

Be yourself. Especially, do not feign affection. Neither be cynical about love; for in the face of all aridity and disenchantment it is perennial as the grass.

Take kindly the counsel of the years, gracefully surrendering the things of youth. Nurture strength of spirit to shield you in sudden misfortune. But do not distress yourself with imaginings. Many fears are born of fatigue and loneliness. Beyond a wholesome discipline, be gentle with yourself.

You are a child of the universe, no less than the trees and the stars. You have a right to be here. And whether or not it is clear to you, no doubt the universe is unfolding as it should.

Therefore be at peace with God, whatever you conceive God to be; and whatever your labors and aspirations, in the noisy confusion of life keep peace with your soul.

With all its sham, drudgery, and broken dreams, it is still a beautiful world. Be careful. Strive to be happy.

Old St. Paul's Church, Baltimore 1692

Benediction

It is now time for us to take our leave of baby Ethan
Whom we shall always remember with great love and affection.
We return to our daily lives more fully with integrity of purpose, cheerfulness and love.
From the midst of our proud mourning we leave this service knowing love is never changed by death, that nothing is ever lost through death
And that in the end, it is the harvest of a new beginning.

Author unknown

And now family and friends it is time to say our farewell to baby Talia

Broken Chain

We little knew the day that
God was going to call your name,
In life we loved you dearly,
in death we do the same.

It broke our hearts to lose you,
but in God we put our trust,
In times as difficult as this,

faith is such a must.
You left us peaceful memories,
your love is still our guide,
And though we cannot see you,
you are always at our side.

Our family chain is broken,
and nothing seems the same,
But as God calls us one by one,
the chain will link again.

Copyright © Ron Tranmer

Committal

Tenderly and reverently we commit the body of precious Ethan to the Universe.
From which all life comes and to which all life, in the end, returns.
We are glad Ethan lived.
We are glad we saw his lovely face so much like his mother and father.
We are glad we held his tiny hand and felt his touch.
We cherish the memory of the joy and beauty he brought to us.

Barry H Young

A Final Prayer

Almighty God and Loving Father
We give thanks for the gift of Your child, Ethan
In faith and trust we leave him in Your keeping,
Praying that in Your good purpose
We may rejoice with him in Your eternal kingdom;
Through Jesus Christ our Lord
Amen

Benediction

In token of our love for Ethan we will resolve to offer a generous affection to each other as far as we are able, and to the young children of humanity the world over.
We leave Ethan in peace and bid him farewell.
More precious than a pearl.
Forever our little boy.

This could be added

Thus in thinking of Talia and in her memory let us promise her to make our lives real and meaningful.
May you find strength and support in your love for one another and may you find peace in your hearts.

A suggestion — hold hands

If graveside service of congregation can leave chapel to outdoors:

And now I ask you to do something really special for Ethan.
Whilst we say farewell would you hold hands with your fellow mourners beside you and let Ethan's spirit, his strength, your sorrow and his love flow through you.
Please join hands.

Each mourner to have a balloon depicting Ethan's chuckle, his tears and his spirit.

Or

The celebrant can say a blessing from one of the above when the family wishes that balloons or pigeons representing the heart, soul, chuckle and tears of their loved child to be let go into the heavens if it is a graveside funeral or the congregation is invited outside of the chapel.

Passage 15 Lest We Forget

The following passages pay tribute to those brave men and women who serve their country in far distant places. What do the words 'Serving one's country' imply? It is to leave all belongings, home and loved ones behind and join others in a fight for ideals and principles. It is considered noble and selfless. It requires commitment, courage and patriotism. Freedom is never a free commodity and has to be fought for or surrendered at much sacrifice. The faith, trust and hope that keeps their spirits alive, cannot be expressed with simple words. Therefore the need to support text with an applicably powerful verse or reading is necessary for the family members. The following verses honour bravery and commitment and pave the way for generosity of spirit.

Before an R S L Service this true story can be told

I would like to tell you a true story. It is a story almost too sacred to be told.

In Kohima in Borneo there stands a huge monolith to the memory of the men of the Second Division of the Australian Army who fell in the battle of Kohima in 1944. In a vast cemetery there are rows and rows of crosses depicting the New Zealand, American and Australian servicemen who gave their lives. On the walls of the monolith are listed the names of the servicemen and across the arch of the monolith is carved an inscription in large letters which reads:

When you go home.
Tell them of us and say
For your tomorrow we gave today

I believe they are the most eloquent words that came out of those terrible tawdry years —

Sixteen simple words — so true — so meaningful — yet so challenging.

Today you and I have all the luxuries of life that one can imagine — we go to the well of life's gifts, its substance, its wealth and its pleasures, and we take from it life's treasures — but forgotten are those who dug the well.

We should never forget who dug that well.

(Name) was one of those who dug the well.

Barry H Young

O Valiant Heart

O Valiant hearts to whom your glory came
Through dust of conflict and through battle flame
Tranquil you lie, your knightly virtue proved
Your memory hallowed in the land you loved
Proudly you gathered, rank on rank to war
As who had heard God's message from afar
All you had hoped for, all you had, you gave
To save mankind — yourselves you scorned to save

Splendid you passed, the great surrender made
Into the light that never more shall fade
Deep your contentment in that blest abode
Who wait the last clear trumpet call of God

From 'O Valiant Hearts' (hymn) — words by John S Arkwright

May They Be Remembered

Some Opening Words

We come together from the diversity of our grieving,
To gather in the warmth of this community.
In times of darkness, there always will be light.
May we hold fast to our convictions
What we do with our lives matters and a caring world is possible after all!

M Maureen Killoran

I Went to See the Soldiers

I went to see the soldiers, row on row on row,
And wondered about each so still, their badges all on show.
What brought them here, what life before
Was like for each of them?
What made them angry, laugh, or cry,
These soldiers, boys and men?
Some so young, some older still, a bond more close than brothers
These men have earned and shared a love, that's not like any others
They trained as one, they fought as one
They shared their last together
That bond endures, that love is true
And will be, now and ever.
I could not know, how could I guess, what choices each had made,
Of how they came to soldiering, what part each one had played.
But here they are and here they'll stay,
Each one silent and in place,
Their headstones line up row on row
They guard this hallowed space.

Copyright © Kenny Martin

Remember Me

Remember me
When I am gone away
Gone far away into the silent land
When you can no more hold me by the hand
Nor I half turn to go, yet turning stay.
Remember me when no more day by day
You tell me of our future that you planned
Only remember me — you understand
It will be late to counsel then or pray.
Yet if you should forget me for awhile
And afterwards remember, do not grieve
For if the darkness and corruption leave
A vestige of the thoughts that once I had
Better by far you should forget and smile
Than that you should remember and be sad.

Christina Rossetti

Ode to the Fallen

In the war-fields of Flanders, the Somme and of France
The poppies are blooming, they sway and they dance
Ten thousand Australians, all tanned and all fit
Have come to this Country, the Jerries to hit.
The guns were all thundering, sombre and dull
The infantry streaming, then so mournful a lull
Our brave boys are falling — courageous and strong
Hark! Something has happened,
Something is wrong!
The Light Horse are stumbling, shaken and falling
They rally their mates on, true to their calling
The battle swords clatter, the foes are retreating
The Aussies press onwards, their mission completing.
So throughout our great country, with pride our hearts turn
Our unknown soldier to us doth return
In the sunshine in Aussie, this day in November
Our Soldiers — our Heroes, we'll always remember!!!!
 Lest we forget!

Barbara Bell

High Flight

Oh! I have slipped the surly bonds of earth
And danced the skies on laughter-silvered wings;
Sunward I've climbed, and joined the tumbling mirth
Of sun-split clouds — and done a hundred things
You have not dreamed of — wheeled and soared and swung
High in the sunlit silence.
Hovering there,
I've chased the shouting wind along, and flung
My eager craft through footless halls of air …
Up, up the long, delirious, burning blue
I've topped the wind-swept heights with easy grace
Where never lark or even eagle flew —
And, while with silent lifting mind I've trod
The high un-trespassed sanctity of space,
Put out my hand and touched the face of God.

John G Magee

In Flanders Fields

In Flanders fields the poppies blow
Between the crosses, row on row,
That mark our place; and in the sky
The larks, still bravely singing, fly
Scarce heard amid the guns below.
We are the Dead. Short days ago
We lived, felt dawn, saw sunset glow,
Loved and were loved
And now we lie in Flanders fields.
Take up our quarrel with the foe:
To you from failing hands we throw
The torch; be yours to hold it high.
If ye break with us who die
We shall not sleep, though poppies grow
In Flanders fields.

Major John McCrae, May 1915

We Will Remember

In the rising of the sun and in its going down,
We will remember him
In the beginning of the year and when it ends,
We will remember him.
When we notice the things he liked,
We will remember him.
When we see in others glimpses of his ways,
We will remember him.
When we see in ourselves things that he would value,
We will remember him.
When we see the example that he set and the difference that he made,
We will remember him.
So as long as we live,
He too will live as we remember him.
Today is a closing and an opening, a saying goodbye and a saying hello again.
So while we say farewell to the (Name) we knew,
We greet the (Name) who has become so much part of us,
The (Name) who lives on with us,
In the thoughts and memories that we will cherish forever.

Adapted from the Litany of Remembrance

We Shall Keep the Faith

Oh! You who sleep in Flanders fields,
Sleep sweet — to rise anew,
We caught the torch you threw,
And holding high we kept
The faith with those who died.
We cherish too, the poppy red
That grows on fields where valour led.
It seems to signal to the skies
That blood of heroes never dies,
But lends a lustre to the red
Of the flower that blooms above the dead
In Flanders' fields.
And now the torch and poppy red
Wear in honour of our dead.
Fear not that ye have died for naught
We've learned the lesson that ye taught
In Flanders' fields.

Author unknown

Please Wear a Poppy

'Please wear a poppy,' the lady said
And held one forth, but I shook my head.
Then I stopped and watched as she offered them there,
And her face was old and lined with care.
But beneath the scars the years had made
There remained a smile that refused to fade.
A boy came whistling down the street,
Bouncing along on carefree feet.
His smile was full of joy and fun,
'Lady,' said he, 'may I have one?'
When she'd pinned it on he turned to say,
'Why do we wear a poppy today?'
The lady smiled in her wistful way
And answered, 'This is Remembrance Day,
And the poppy there is the symbol for
The gallant men who died in war.
And because they did, you and I are free —
That's why we wear a poppy, you see.'
I had a boy about your size,
With golden hair and big blue eyes.
He loved to play and jump and shout,
Free as a bird he would race about.
As the years went by he learned and grew
and became a man — as you will, too.
He was fine and strong, with a boyish smile,
But he'd seemed with us such a little while
When war broke out and he went away.
I still remember his face that day
When he smiled at me and said, "Goodbye,
I'll be back soon, Mom, so please don't cry."
But the war went on and he had to stay,

And all I could do was wait and pray.
His letters told of the awful fight,
(I can see it still in my dreams at night),
With the tanks and guns and cruel barbed wire,
And the mines and bullets, the bombs and fire.
Till at last, at last, the war was won —
And that's why we wear a poppy, son.'
The small boy turned as if to go,
Then said, 'Thanks, lady, I'm glad to know.
That sure did sound like an awful fight,
But your son — did he come back all right?'
A tear rolled down each faded cheek.
She shook her head, but didn't speak.
I slunk away in a sort of shame,
And if you were me you'd have done the same,
For our thanks, in giving, is oft delayed,
Though our freedom was bought — and thousands paid!
And so when we see a poppy worn,
Let us reflect on the burden borne,
By those who gave their very all
When asked to answer their country's call
That we at home in peace might live.
Then wear a poppy! Remember — and give!

Don Crawford

From the Rubaiyat

Ah, make the most of what we yet may spend
Before we too into the Dust descend
Dust unto Dust, and under Dust, to lie
Sans Wine, sans Song, sans Singer, and — sans End.

The Moving Finger

The moving finger writes, and, having writ
Moves on — nor all thy Piety nor Wit
Shall lure it back to cancel half a Line,
Nor all thy Tears wash out a word of it.

Omar Khayyam (Edward Fitzgerald's translation)

Farewell

Shadows, fall upon the world of my loved ones
They, no longer see the dew upon the rose
The sun has slipped behind a darkened rain cloud
Their souls are clenched in pain, as sorrow grows.
From the surface of their minds — they have set forth
Setting each daily chore, with melancholy face
That yields no more, no less than asked —
And yet, I long to reach right out, and say aloud —
'Cry not for me, my friends, hear the music in my heart
And kiss my memory — Farewell!'
I have lived, so well upon this earth
I have followed, many paths that reached the sun
If I had troubles, or pain, or heartaches —
I cherished more the smiles, a thousand more, when one —

Had said to me in friendship — 'I wish you well'
They were sweet words I treasured long.
To the hilltops, to the clouds, to the moon and stars beyond
To a pasture — glistening with fresh rain — I run
So, cry not for me, my friends, hear the music in my heart
And kiss my memory — 'Farewell!'

They did not die in haste, they passed on — victoriously

An Anzac Tribute

They rose and fought as one, shedding
their childhood — gloriously

Leaving their families, wives and friends
they marched on — fearlessly

Making the fight for freedom their
cause — intentionally

They lay in ditches cold and weary
shielding each other — continuously

They braved the enemy, in tortured
pain — enduringly

They gave their lives so we
may live — courageously.

Passage 16 Peace after Suffering

The following passages can be used when someone has lost their lives to drugs, illness, tragic accident, and even for the lonely. They can be adapted to suit that particular sad occasion.

A lonely person with no family

And here I would like to read to you a reading about friendship and I dedicate this to all of you who were a friend to Warren, for as you know he had no family.

Thank you for being a friend to me when needing someone there.
My failing hopes to bolster and my secret fears to share.
Thank you for being so good to me when it was hard to know the wisest course to follow, what to do and where to go.
Thank you for giving me confidence when I needed a helping hand
Speaking the word that led me through the course of the day.
Thank you for all you did and said to ease the weight for me
Never intruding but always there in the background, helping quietly.
Thank you not only for sympathy in times of grief and stress — but for all you have meant to me in terms of happiness.

Author unknown

Another poem for a lonely person

Why should we be in such haste to succeed
And in such desperate enterprises
If a man does not keep pace with his companions,
Perhaps it is because he hears a different drummer.
Let him step to the music which he hears,
However treasured or far away.

Henry David Thoreau

For a Friend

I loved my friend.
He went away from me.
There's nothing more to say.
The poem ends,
Soft as it began — I loved my friend.

Langston Hughes

Slow Dance

Have you ever watched kids
On a merry-go-round?
Or listened to the rain
Slapping on the ground?
Ever followed a butterfly's erratic flight?
Or gazed at the sun into the fading night?
You better slow down.
Don't dance so fast.
Time is short.
The music won't last.
Do you run through each day
On the fly?
When you ask How are you?
Do you hear the reply?
When the day is done!
Do you lie in your bed
With the next hundred chores
Running through your head?
You'd better slow down
Don't dance so fast.

Time is short.
The music won't last.
Ever told your child,
We'll do it tomorrow?
And in your haste,
Not see his sorrow?
Ever lost touch,
Let a good friendship die
Cause you never had time
To call and say, 'Hi'

You'd better slow down.
Don't dance so fast.
Time is short.
The music won't last.
When you run so fast to get somewhere
You miss half the fun of getting there.
When you worry and hurry through your day,
It is like an unopened gift.
Thrown away.

Life is not a race.
Do take it slower
Hear the music
Before the song is over.

Author unknown

For someone who has suffered from Alzheimer's

The Shadow of a Man

How do you cope when someone you hold
Most dear — suddenly dies?
How do you face people, aloof, detached?
Yet mourn in silence — with unheard cries
How do you hold back the tears?
Yet folks think you're very brave
But you battle on with daily tasks
Dwelling on comforts he once gave
How do you express the hurt, the shame?
When recognition faded … even his name.
He used to laugh, whistle and hum
Appreciate music, movies and lots of fun
Then floundered helplessly … misunderstood!
You then coped — as best you could
How do you say, you had to repeat
Patiently — things one takes for granted?
As he once housed goodness and beauty
That God had initially planted.
Each time you caressed his feeble hand
Only those who care — may understand …
He'd lost every goal; it tore your soul
That saddened, empty hole …
The laughter, the songs, the games once played
Memories of yesterday — still heavy with pain
Can never be erased …
As the Love you felt and the Love you still feel
Will always, always remain the same!

For one who has lost his/her life to drugs

(For someone who has been ill for many years)
(Inspired by the Book 'April Fool's Day' by Bryce Courtney)

One So beloved

Through vacant wastelands, love remains
And memories rustle the pages of one sweet life
The unanswered 'whys?' That were uttered
In frustrated plea, so frequently
Whilst loving hearts perceived he was special
And his life had cruel limitations!
In a kaleidoscope of pills and potions he manifested
Light and dark, fire and water, understanding, ambition
Persuasion and perseverance
Acknowledging neither defeat nor self-pity
Steadfastly pursuing excellence
His youth disappearing in molten dreams
'Twixt days awash with tears and silent pain
An odyssey of pierced veins and bruised seams
Yet his smiles belied the turbulence!
Though small, he stood so very tall with countenance
That masked a tortured spirit
Thus bravely, loving expansively, 'midst the miasma
Of drips and drugs and alien hospice
He clung to hope, but his stay on earth was done
And peace — his rightful due!
A camouflage of mindless hours and anguished minutes
Once fettered, springing free, as patterned lives
Strive on — another page is turned
Come, kiss all strife goodbye and smile
For having known him!

Tragic Accident

Life does proceed when a loved one leaves.
But it's difficult for us who are left behind
We'll pick ourselves up and try again,
We'll make the effort to function again.
It won't be easy, as we all know.
But we won't give up — the change made us grow.
We loved (Name) so much, and fate was unkind.
She/he went away first, she/he left us behind.
The pain in our hearts will remain yet awhile.
But yesterday's gone, tomorrow we'll try to smile.

Author unknown

Goodbye My Friend

Though we never know
Where life will take us,
I know it's just a ride
On the wheel.
And we never know
When death will shake us
And we wonder how
It will feel.
So goodbye my friend.
I know I'll never see you again.
But the time together
Through all the years
Will take away these tears.
It's OK now — goodbye my friend.
I see a lot of things

That make me crazy,
And I guess I held on to you.
You could have run away
And left well maybe,
But it wasn't time
And we both knew.
So goodbye my friend.
I know I'll never see you again.
But the love you gave me
Through all the years
Will take away these tears.
I'm OK now — goodbye my friend.

Author unknown

Passage 17 Miscellaneous

The following miscellaneous collection of unusual and heartfelt poems may be used to suit appropriate situations. The very powerful and moving poem of love and unbearable loss, *Stop All the Clocks, Cut Off the Telephone* (otherwise known as *Funeral Blues*), is on page 178. This is accompanied by several humorous, religious and sad poems, including *Crossing the Bar* by Alfred, Lord Tennyson.

The Swaggie

St Peter put his quart pot down and rubbed his saintly eyes
As through the clouds came a figure bowed, pursued by hordes of flies.
He came tramping up to Heaven's Gate and stood there in amaze
He dropped his swag and tucker bag and said, 'Well, spare me days!
I've humped this old Matilda since the age of seventeen,
There's not a track in the great outback that we two haven't seen.
So when I rolled me final swag I thought I'd cleaned the slate
But stone the crows, before me nose, I sees another gate!

'In fifty years of tramping and covering all the while
Twelve miles a day — at least to say, with two gates to the mile.
I'm not much good at figures but the way I calculate
In my career I've opened near on fifty thousand gates.
'There was gates that fairly haunt me, there was gates of every sort.
Sagging gates and dragging gates, high, low, long and short.
Gates that seemed to challenge you and gates that seemed to grin.
Lazy gates and crazy gates that hung by half a hinge.

'Gates tied up with fencing wire and gates with fancy scrolls,
With patent catch and homemade latch, and gates made out of poles.
Wide gates and narrow gates, big barriers and small,
Rusted gates and busted gates; I've wrestled with them all.
'Now I've opened them and shut them, till the sight of all I hate,
And I'd sooner miss your Heavenly bliss than open that there gate.
'What's that you say? You'll open it? Well, that's what I call nice.
And close it, too, when I get through?
This must be Paradise.'

Author unknown

A little ditty which can be used for a wag that has passed

Go On — Say It Now ...

If with pleasure you are viewing
Any work that I am doing
If you like me or love me — tell me now.
Don't withhold your approbation
Till the parson makes ovation
And I lie with snowy lilies o'er my brow
For no matter how you shout it
I won't care a damn about it
I'll not know how many teardrops you have shed
If you think some credit's due me
Now's the time to slip it to me
For I cannot read my tombstone when I'm dead

Author unknown

Untitled

Time is too slow for those who wait
Too swift for those who fear
Too long for those who grieve, too short for those who rejoice
But for those who rejoice, but for those who live, time is eternity
Hours fly, flowers die, new days, new ways pass by, love says

Author unknown

The Gate of the Year

And I said to the man who stood at the gate of the year:
'Give me a light, that I may tread safely into the unknown!'
And he replied:
'Go out into the darkness and put your hand into the hand of God.
That shall be to you better than light and safer than a known way.'
So, I went forth, and finding the Hand of God,
Trod gladly into the night.
And He led me toward the hills and the breaking of day in the lone east
So, heart be still!
What need our little life,
Our human life, to know,
If God hath comprehension?
In all the dizzy strife
Of things both high and low
God hideth his intention.

M Louise Haskins

Thought for the Day

Love is a force more formidable than any other.
It is invisible. It cannot be seen or measured.
Yet it is powerful enough to transform you in a moment
And offer you more joy than any material possession could.

Crossing the Bar

Sunset and evening star,
And one clear call for me!
And may there be no moaning of the bar,
When I put out to sea,

But such a tide as moving seems asleep,
Too full for sound and foam,
When that which drew from out the boundless deep
Turns again home.

Twilight and evening bell,
And after the dark!
And may there be no sadness of farewell,
When I embark;

For tho' from out our bourne of Time and Place
The flood may bear me far,
I hope to see my Pilot face to face
When I have crost the bar.

Alfred, Lord Tennyson

Stop All the Clocks, Cut Off the Telephone

Stop all the clocks, cut off the telephone,
Prevent the dog from barking with a juicy bone,
Silence the pianos and with muffled drum
Bring out the coffin, let the mourners come.

Let aeroplanes circle moaning overhead
Scribbling on the sky the message — He is Dead,
Put the crepe bows around the white necks of the public doves,
Let the traffic policemen wear black cotton gloves.

He was my North, my South, my East and West,
My working week and my Sunday rest,
My moon, my midnight, my talk, my song;
I thought that love would last forever: I was wrong.

The stars are not wanted now: put out every one;
Pack up the moon and dismantle the sun;
Pour away the ocean and sweep away the wood.
For nothing now can ever come to any good.

I Am Not There

Do not stand at my grave and weep I am not there
I do not sleep I am a thousand winds that blow
I am the diamond glints on snow
I am the sunlight on ripened grain
I am the gentle autumn rain
When you awaken in the morning's hush
I am the swift uplifting rush
Of quiet birds
In circled flight
I am the soft stars that shine at night
Do not stand at my grave and cry.
I am not there; I did not die

Author unknown

As a tribute to Ted

Trees

I think that I shall never see
A poem lovely as a tree.
A tree whose hungry mouth is prest
Against the earth's sweet flowing breast.
A tree that looks at God all day
And lifts her leafy arms to pray.
A tree that may in summer wear
A nest of robins in her hair.
Upon whose bosom snow has lain
Who intimately lives with rain.
Poems are made by fools like me.
But only God can make a tree.

Joyce Kilmer

Mother Theresa wrote some beautiful words about life which illustrate the life lived by Helen

Life is an opportunity, welcome it.
Life is beauty, admire it.
Life is a beatitude, savour it.
Life is a dream, make it a reality.
Life is a challenge, face it.
Life is a duty, accomplish it.
Life is a game, play it.
Life is precious, take care of it.
Life is wealth, preserve it.

Life is love, enjoy it.
Life is a mystery, discover it.
Life is a promise, fulfil it.
Life is sadness, overcome it.
Life is a hymn, sing it.
Life is a struggle, accept it.
Life is an adventure, risk it.
Life is happiness, treasure it.

Mother Theresa

Geoff was one with the bush, its freedom, its beauty, the scent of the gum
and the following is a poem written for Geoff

I Have an Understanding with the Bush

I have an understanding with the bush.
By day when sprayed with golden sun.
By night when hushed in silver light.
Its trees, its brush, its birds, its hollows and its peaks reach out at me,
Its secrets shared on whispering winds.
For I am one with them and they with me.

Barry H Young

Abou Ben Adhem

Abou Ben Adhem (may his tribe increase!)
Awoke one night from a deep dream of peace,
And saw, within the moonlight in his room,
Making it rich, and like a lily in bloom,
An Angel writing in a book of gold.

Exceeding peace had made Ben Adhem bold,
And to the Presence in the room he said,
'What writest thou?' — The vision raised its head,
And with a look made all sweet accord,
Answered, 'The names of those who love the Lord.'

'And is mine one?' said Abou. 'Nay not so',
Replied the Angel, Abou spoke more low,
But cheerily still, and said, 'I pray thee then,
Write me as one who loves his fellow man.'

The Angel wrote and vanished. The next night
It came again with a great wakening light,
And showed the names whom love of God had bless'd,
And lo! Ben Adhem's name led all the rest.

James Henry Leigh Hunt

A Reflection on an Autumn's Day

I took up a handful of grain and let it slip flowing through my fingers, and I said to myself: 'This is what it is all about. There is no longer any room for pretence. At harvest time the essence is revealed — the straw and chaff are set aside; they have done their job. The grain alone matters — sacks of pure gold.'

So it is when a person dies, the essence of that person is revealed. At the moment of death a person's character stands out happily for the person who has forged it well over the years. Then it will not be the great achievement that will matter, or, how much money or possessions a person has amassed. These like the straw and the chaff, will be left behind. It is what he has made of himself that will matter. Death can take away from us what we have, but it cannot rob us of who we are.

Author unknown

No Funeral Gloom

No funeral gloom, my dears, when I am gone,
corpse-gazing, tears, black raiment, graveyard grimness.
Think of me as withdrawn into the dimness,
yours still, you mine.
Remember all the best of our past moments,
and forget the rest;
and so to where I wait, come gently on.

William Allingham

Things I left Unsaid

Family o' mine:
I should like to send you a sunbeam or the twinkle of some bright star
or a tiny piece of the downy fleece that clings to a cloud afar.
I should like to send you the essence of myriad sun-kissed flowers
or the lilting song as it floats along, of a brook through fairy bowers.
I should like to send you the dew-drops that glisten at break of day
and then at night the eerie light that mantles the Milky Way.
I should like to send you the power that nothing can overthrow —
the power to smile and laugh the while a-journeying through life you go.
But these are mere fanciful wishes; I'll send you a Godspeed instead
and I'll clasp your hand — then you'll understand all the things I have left
unsaid.

Author unknown

For Katrina's Sun Dial

Time is too slow for those who wait,
Too swift for those who fear,
Too long for those who grieve,
Too short for those who rejoice,
But for those who love, time is
Eternity.

Henry van Dyke (1852-1933)
Read by Lady Jane Fellowes at Princess Diana's funeral.

Life Is But a Stopping Place

Life is but a stopping place,
A pause in what's to be,
A resting place along the road,
to sweet eternity.
We all have different journeys.
Different paths along the way …
We all were meant to learn some things,
but never meant to stay …
Our destination is a place,
Far greater than we know.
For some the journey's quicker,
For some the journey's slow.
And when the journey finally ends,
We'll claim a great reward,
And find an everlasting peace,
Together with the Lord.

Author unknown

A reading for a passionate fisherman

Gone Fishin'

I've finished life's chores assigned to me,
So put me on a boat headed out to sea.
Please send along my fishin' pole
For I've been invited to the fishin' hole.

Where every day is a day to fish.
To fill your heart with every wish,
Don't worry, or feel sad for me,
I'm fishin' with the Master of the sea.

We will miss each other for a while.
But will you come and bring your smile
That won't be long you will see,
Till we're together you and me.

To all of those who think of me,
Be happy as I go out to sea,
If others wonder why I'm missin'
Just tell them I've gone fishin'

D Pepper

A reading for a passionate bowler

A Bowler's Prayer

I ask God's blessing, as I bowl,
That He, my game will bless,
I ask not for a higher score,
But strength to do my best.
I ask, that I might concentrate
On fundamental things,
So I'll achieve consistency
That only practice brings.
That He will still my shakiness,
And dry my sweaty palm;
That he will grant me confidence,
And give me peace and calm.
But more than this, help me to show
More friendliness and love;
For I know my strength and confidence,
Is a gift from God above.

Ray Prillwitz

In the Funeral Celebrant's Handbook you will find services for Returned Serviceman, R S L, Serviceman and Woman, Legatee, Memorial and a prayer for a Rotary Service. The author has had many requests for an appropriate Rotary Service to be conducted in honour of a deceased Rotarian.

Rotary Funeral Service Barry H Young

The Clergyman or Celebrant will invite the President of the member's Rotary Club or its nominee to come forward to conduct the service.

Clergyman or Celebrant to say —

'Ladies and Gentlemen I welcome you to honour and celebrate the life of (Name) our distinguished and honoured member of the Rotary Club of (Place) to conduct this Rotary Service today.

'In honour of their deceased member, President (Name) of the Rotary Club of (Place) will now conduct a Rotary Service.'

The President will say some words about the deceased's role in Rotary.

The President will announce the aims and objectives of Rotary.

'The object of Rotary is to encourage and foster the ideal of service as a basis of worthy enterprise and, in particular, to encourage and foster the development of acquaintance as an opportunity for service. It is an organisation of business and professional persons united worldwide who provide humanitarian service, encourage high ethical standards in all vocations, business and professions and help build goodwill and peace in the world.'

The President will ask all Rotarians in the congregation to stand and repeat after him — The Four-Way Test.

1 Is it the truth?
2 Is it fair to all concerned?
3 Will it build goodwill and better friendships?
4 Will it be beneficial to all concerned?

The President asks all Rotarians to be seated.

The President then proceeds to the coffin to place the deceased's Rotary Club flag on the coffin.

The President returns to the lectern to say — 'I now ask you to observe a minute's silence in memory of our member (Name).'

The service to conclude with the Rotary Prayer.

The President to say — 'As a tribute to (Name) I will now read the Rotary Prayer.'

A Rotary Prayer

Let Us Pray

Eternal spirit, from whom we come, to whom we belong, and in whose presence is our peace and joy, grant us now such spiritual triumph in the memory of our fellow Rotarian, (Name), in whose character and service we rejoice.

We thank you for the Rotary Club of (Place) and the opportunities it gave him to fulfil his desires to serve the common good.

We are grateful for the friends we have made, the fellowship we enjoy, the accomplishments for the happiness of others; and we acknowledge the sincere and active part that (Name) has played in the enjoyment of those benefits.

In Rotary's ideal of service 'Service above Self', we commit ourselves anew to —

Truth in word and deed
Fairness to all concerned
Goodwill and better stronger friendships
Beneficence to all concerned

And we also pray for humility in your power, strength in our weakness, dignity in service, guidance in our movements, and your blessing in our plannings
For your love's sake
Amen

Reverend David Ryrie and Reverend Geoff Browne

The Rotary Club President hands back to the Clergyman or Celebrant conducting the funeral service.

Note:
The President or his Club's nominee conduct the service.

I have added the words highlighted to the prayer written by — Rev David Ryrie and the Rev Geoff Browne who have given me their acceptance to use.

Passage 18 Peace Perfect Peace

A suicide, or, as some may say, 'ending one's life', is one of the hardest funeral services for a celebrant to conduct. The taking of one's own life is a decision often made by someone who is lonely, heartbroken, suffering from a debilitating illness or a drug addiction or is emotionally defeated or unstable. Of course there could be other reasons. The celebrant will be aware that for the families the situation is often incomprehensible and that they will be feeling heart-wrenching disbelief and a terrible numbness. The aftermath too may be emotionally crippling; sometimes families experience feelings of guilt. They may feel devastated by the immediate loss and unable to cope; they may be angry or withdrawn. It is therefore up to the celebrant to arrange, direct and assist in order to effectively provide a healing or acceptable leave taking. I hope the following may assist your search in providing the perfect verse.

I Leave ... It Is My Time

I need to leave, no anguish, no trace of being
Of having unreservedly experienced and loved
I must not tarry, nor linger for the final scene
As I was never 'comfy' with any saddened word
I need to fly this land, leave no imprint on sand
As silently as a whisper, without sign — unheard
Turn pages in an Album — if you must
Remember with a smile, but leave no frame
As comprehension of the 'once that was'
Would unsuspectingly — freely gather dust
Do not fear for me, as I have severed earthly ties
I cannot change or trick the mechanism
Nor ponder on the contrite 'might have been'
As I — just I — perceived what lay before my eyes.
Wrong or Right — I was my 'jury', it would seem
No feigned regret or impassioned woe implore
It's time to leave — I now entreat you please
Say 'Farewell' and softly close the door!

Copyright © Ruth Van Gramberg

Let Go and Say Goodbye

The memories of you, our son, will never die,
Even though you chose to close your eyes.
Our love for you lives on, our son,
Just as we chose to go on living as one.
Maybe you did give us a gift unknowingly
And that is to learn to live again — fully and completely.
The pain of losing you will always be there.
But there comes a time to let go and say goodbye.
In our hearts you will stay forever and a day.
Farewell, we'll love you always.

Author unknown,
The Compassionate Friends *(Victoria) Magazine, 2003*

If

We thought that you were happy,
We must have been blind,
We knew that you were suffering,
But we didn't know your mind,
You left our hearts all aching,
And we don't know how to cope,
If we had talked it over,
There might have been some hope.

Author unknown

In Liberating Breeze

I soar above in spacious skies; I lift my spirits with glee
And swift above the clouds I rise; life's shackles bursting free
Above the emerald brooks and ferns, skimming through dappled shadows
Beyond majestic gums and terns, careering across the meadows
Bitter constraints, bruised ego unleashed
Far-reaching goals or glorious deeds
I flee this earth's stringencies with ease
The ultimate joy I now embrace — the purity of space
In liberating breeze …

A gentle mist upon my brow, soft sunlight spangles my hair
A kaleidoscopic flight so bright, on my new freedom thoroughfare
So strong my soul, my heart so light, this fresh buoyancy perceive
As waters blue and scintillating waves, whisper softly, beckoning me
I've tarried long and wearily,
traipsing bravely hidden chasms and meads
I flee this earth's stringencies with ease
The ultimate joy I now embrace — the purity of space
In liberating breeze …

A meaningful reading

It takes time to accept a loss, particularly one that is so unexpected. In time sorrow may lessen, wounds may heal; however, importantly, the most valuable feature that remains will be your memories, your love, and the special moments you shared. Nicole has reached the end of her journey here on earth. With admiration, we acknowledge her laughter; with a smile we acknowledge her sense of humour. With gratitude we acknowledge her determined spirit and passion for living and with love we thank her for sharing our lives ...

Author unknown

Beautiful memories are like priceless art,
Pictures to treasure that shine in the heart
Like beautiful roses, they will never die
Their beauty lives on in the beholder's eye.
Beautiful memories of someone you love
Will comfort and lift like the wings of a dove
For in beautiful dreams there is no less pain
In beautiful memories — you are together again.

Passage 19 In God's Loving Care

Religion plays an important role in many people's lives and consequently, religious ceremonies and rituals are traditionally part of life's important milestones. Listed are the most common and appropriate bible readings for a religious service conducted by a celebrant.

Suitable Scripture Readings

1 Corinthians — C 13 — verses 1 to 13 — Faith, hope and love

2 Corinthians — C 4 — verses 1 to 16 — Things eternal

2 Corinthians — C5 — verse 10 — Living by faith and hope

Isaiah — C54 — verse 10 — For the mountains may depart.

John — C14 — verses 1 to 6 — Let not your heart be troubled

John — C 5 — verses 19 to 25 — Power to give life

John — C 6 — verses 35 to 40 — Jesus the bread of life

John — C 11 — verses 17 to 27 — Jesus the resurrection and the life

Mark — C 10 — verses 13 to 16 — Jesus blesses little children

Matthew — C 5 — verses 1 to 12 — True happiness

Matthew — C5 — verses 28 to 30 — Come to me, all who labour

Psalm 46 — verses 1 to 3 — God is our refuge and strength

Psalm 25 — verses 1 — 11 — To you O Lord I lift up my soul

Philippians — C3 — verses 10 to16 and 20 to 21 — God's purpose for us

Revelations — C21 — verses 1 to 7 — The new heaven and earth

Romans — C14 — verses 7 to 9 — We belong to the Lord

1 Thessalonians — C 4 — verses 13 to 18 — The coming of the Lord

Concluding Thoughts

We do not have to rely
upon memories
to recapture the spirit
of those we have loved and lost —
they live within our souls
in some perfect sanctuary
which even death
cannot destroy —

Acknowledgements

The author and the publisher gratefully acknowledge the following persons/organisations for the use of their written materials:

References

Dally R Messenger, selected text reproduced and adapted with kind permission from the author, from his book *Ceremonies and Celebrations: Vows, Tributes and Readings*, Publisher: Lothian, Melbourne, 1999) Copyright © Dally Messenger.

Anzac Tribute from *Kissed by the Sun* (Publisher: K&R Publishers 1997) Copyright © Ruth Gramberg.

One So Beloved, Passage of Time, In Liberating Breeze, Goodbye Little One, Shadow of a Man, Cry Not for Me, Memories, I Miss You, You Left Behind from *Little Pebbles and Stepping Stones* (The Australian Federation of Civil Celebrants 2005) Copyright © Ruth Gramberg.

Jason's Gift from Love Never Dies: A Mother's Journey from Loss to Love (Jodere 2002) Copyright © Sandy Goodman.

'We do not have to rely', from the *Thoughts of Nanushka Vols X1-X11*. Copyright © NAN WITCOMB Oct. 1985.

Is presently in The Thoughts of Nanushka Vols V11-X11. Copyright © NAN WITCOMB 1987.

Pages/Poems/Prose

Page 6: Reinhold Niebuhr, *Serenity Prayer*; Page 11: Bessie A Stanley, *That Man Is a Success* adapted from *What Constitutes Success*; Page 12: Lisa Wroble, *You are Stronger than You Think* adapted from *Within You Is the Strength to Meet Life's Challenges*; Christina Rossetti (the following two poems), Page 19: *Do Not Grieve*, Page 156: *Remember Me*; Page 20: Copyright © Nancy Wood, *Untitled*; Page 21: S Hall Young, *Untitled*; Copyright © Ruth Van Gramberg (the following twenty-six poems/prayers), Page 25: *Remember Me in Your Hearts*, Page 31: *Memories*, Page 37: *Untimely Loss*, Page 39: *Five Candles*, Page 41: *I Miss You*, Page 51: *My Mother*, Page 52: *My Children*, Page 53: *Canvas of My Love*, Page 54: *Being Part of a Family*, Page 60: *Give the Love in Me Away*, Page 61: *When Life Comes to an End*, Page 96: *One So Beloved*, Page 97: *In Leaving You Behind*, Page 98: *Passage of Time*, Page 99: *Cry Not for Me*, Page 109: *The warmth of her love* (No title), Page 115: *Parental Prayer: From a Loving Mother*, Page 129: *You Left Without Saying Goodbye*, Page 130: *Goodbye Little One*, Page 164: *Farewell*, Page 165: *An Anzac Tribute*, Page 170: *The Shadow of a Man*, Page 171: *One So Beloved*, Page 191: *I Leave … It Is My Time*, Page 193: *In Liberating Breeze*; Page 28: Isla Paschal Richardson, *To Those I Love*; Page 29: Mary Lee Hall, *Turn Again to Life*; Page 31: AK Rowswell, *Should You Go First*; Page 36: Walter Rinder, *Finding You in Beauty*; Page 38: Simon Bridges, *Tomorrows*; Page 46: Diane Robertson, *Are You There?*; Page 47: Copyright © Linda P Stauffer, *My Beloved Katie*; Page 48: Copyright © Sandy Goodman, *Jason's Gift*; Pamela M Brooke (the following two poems), Page 65: *The One I Was*, Page 65: *Journey's End*; Page 66: Copyright © Maggie Dent, *Sometimes*; Page 71: RL Stephenson, *Requiem*; Page 71: Anne Bronte, *Farewell*; Page 72: Mary Elizabeth Frye, *Graveside*; Copyright © Wendy Haynes (the following three pieces), Page 81: *Deep Peace*, Page 103: *We honour the life of …*; Page 116: *May peace soothe your heart and mind …*; Page 82: Yvonne Goddard, *Imagine*; Page 83: Canon Henry Scott Holland, *Death Is Nothing at All*; Page 86: Rabindranath Tagore, *Farewell My Friends*; Page 87: Amelia Josephine Burr, *A Song of Living*; Page 89: Ellen Brenneman, *Her Journey's Just Begun*; Page 93: Charles Henry Bent, *You can shed tears now that Jason has gone* (No title);

Page 94: Grace Noll Crowell, *Let Me Come In*; Page 100: Domenic Vincenzo Ferrari, *Heaven's Stairs*; Page 103: Copyright © Dally Messenger, *Tenderly and reverently ...* (No title); Page 104: Dorothy McRae-McMahon, *The first truth is that nothing is lost in the universe... (No title)*; Copyright © Sarah York (the following two readings from *Remembering Well*), Page 107: *The act is done. The words have been said.* (No title), Page 112: *Ashes to ashes, Dust to dust*; Peter Marshall (the following two readings), Page 122: A *Prayer for Bereavement*, Page 123: *A Prayer for One Who Will Not Be Comforted*; Page 125: Kahlil Gibran, from *The Prophet*; Page 135: Edgar Guest, *Child Loaned*; Page 137: John Foster, *Sleep Soft*; Page 138: Cindy O'Connor, *When God calls little children to dwell with him above* (No title); Page 145: Frank Brown, *Sometimes, When the Sun Goes Down*; Page 146: Barbara Carlson, *A Prayer for Parents*; Page 148: Copyright © Ron Tranmer, *Broken Chain*; Page 154: John S Arkwright, *O Valiant Hearts*; Page 154: Maureen Killoran, *We come together from the diversity of our grieving...* (No title); Page 155: Copyright © Kenny Martin, *I Went to See the Soldiers*; Page 157: Barbara Bell, *Ode to the Fallen*; Page 158: John G Magee, *High Flight*; Page 159: Major John McCrae, *In Flanders Fields*; Page 162: Don Crawford, *Please Wear a Poppy*; Omar Khayyam (the following two readings), Page 164: From *The Rubaiyat*, Page 164: *The Moving Finger*; Page 167: Henry David Thoreau, *Why should we be in such haste to succeed...* (No title); Page 168: Langston Hughes, *For a Friend*; Page 177: M Louise Haskins, *The Gate of the Year*; Page 177: Copyright © Dr Barbara De Angelis, Ph.D., *Thought for the Day*; Page 178: Alfred, Lord Tennyson, *Crossing the Bar*; Page 178: Copyright © WH Auden, *Stop All the Clocks, Cut Off the Telephone (or The Funeral Blues)*; Page 180: Joyce Kilmer, *Trees*; Page 180: Mother Theresa, *Life is an opportunity, welcome it ...* (No title); Page 182: James Henry Leigh Hunt, *Abou Ben Adhem*; Page 183: William Allingham, *No Funeral Gloom*; Page 184: Henry van Dyke, *For Katrina's Sun Dial*; Page 186: D Pepper, *Gone Fishin'*; Page 187: Ray Prillwitz, *A Bowler's Prayer*; Page 189: Reverend David Ryrie and Reverend Geoff Browne, *And we also pray for humility in your power ...* (to add to Rotary prayer); Page 197: Copyright © Nan Witcomb, *We do not have to rely ...*

Several of the poems and prayers have been written or adapted by the author Barry H Young. There are also numerous pieces where the author is unknown.

Every effort has been made by the author and the publisher to trace and acknowledge copyright and obtain relevant permissions. Should any infringement of copyright have occurred we would be happy to rectify this in any further edition. Please contact the publisher at the address at the front of this book.

Thanks from the Author

My sincere and heartfelt thanks to all whose valuable contributions helped to make this book a reality.

I acknowledge and extend my thanks to JoJo Publishing and its team of talented professionals, who, following a successful national and global journey across oceans and skies marketing the 'Funeral Celebrant's Handbook', encouraged me to write a sequel.

Thank you to all of those magnificent poets whose prose and verse helped paint these pages — names revered, those lesser known and some anonymous — for the music, warmth and heart-stirring magic portrayed.

Especially, I extend my gratitude to Ruth Van Gramberg, a treasured friend and Australia's finest poet, for her assistance in breathing life into a solemn subject and who shared my vision for this book; she has been an inspiration! Her many poems capture the tenderness, anguish and depth of emotions experienced in the loss of a loved one. Thank you, Ruth.

My thanks go to Chameleon Print Design for the striking design of the cover and book.

To my editor, Ormé Harris — a true professional, who has overseen her mission and my quest to provide 'Saying Farewell to Those We Love'. Thank you, Ormé.

This book is dedicated to the above-mentioned and to all practising and aspiring celebrants who have been entrusted with the gift of responsibility and professional duty of composing and conducting each beautiful and meaningful funeral service. It is a privilege and honour to wear the title of Funeral Celebrant.